Culinary Arts Institute

CROCKERY COOKING

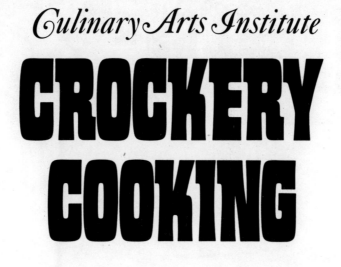

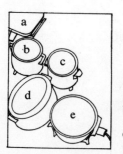

Featured in cover photo:
a. **Rosé Baked Apples,** 94
b. **Split Pea Soup,** 24
c. **Multi-Vegetable Beef Stew,** 32
d. **Roast Stuffed Turkey,** 69
e. **Super Turban Cake,** 85

CROCKERY

CROCKERY COOKING

The Culinary Arts Institute Staff:

Helen Geist: Director
Sherrill Corley and Barbara MacDonald: Editors
Ethel La Roche: Editorial Assistant • Ivanka Simatic: Recipe Tester
Edward Finnegan: Executive Editor • Malinda Miller: Copy Editor
Charles Bozett: Art Director • John Mahalek: Art Assembly

Book designed and coordinated by Charles Bozett and Laurel DiGangi

Illustrations by Gwen Connelly

COOKING

Adventures in Cooking SERIES

Culinary Arts Institute

1727 South Indiana Avenue, Chicago, Illinois 60616

FOREWORD

In this jet age, why all the excitement about the slow-cooking pot? While the rest of the world rushes on, it takes its own sweet time, producing dishes reminiscent of a more leisurely past.

To find out, Culinary Arts Institute has spent several months putting crocks to the test. Twenty models simmered away in our Test Kitchen, and members of our staff tested at home to see how well they suit the life of the working woman.

The crock's main advantage, we feel, is that it turns out dishes with old-fashioned goodness while adjusting cooking time to suit the cook. Once the food is in the pot and the control turned to Low, you can leave it to its own devices. And you needn't hurry back; dinner will be ready and waiting when you want it.

Just as the watched pot never boils, the unwatched slow cooker never burns. The heat on Low is steady, and the environment is moist because the steam can't escape. Under these conditions, an extension of an hour or so won't harm the food.

Moist heat offers an important fringe benefit—economy. In combination with expanded cooking times, it will tenderize the very cuts of meat that cost the least. It may not be the pot of gold waiting at the end of your rainbow, but it could mean a little left over in the food budget.

During hot weather the crock lets you cook without heating up the kitchen. Stews, soups, pot roasts, quick breads, and cakes—usually reserved for wintry weather—become year-round possibilities.

The slow cooker is a handy hostess tool; it doubles as a keep-warm serving dish. At holiday time a pot of wassail or glögg can simmer away on the buffet without taking up precious space on the range top.

Whether or not it is the all-purpose cooker that some claim is a matter of personal opinion. Some of our testers were enthusiastic about the baked goods from the crock; others thought they'd use it exclusively for soups, stews, and stocks. Few thought they'd take the time to prepare stew ingredients before leaving for work.

We believe that the slow cooker may have gained an unjustified reputation for being a work saver. While it is true that it lets you adjust cooking schedules to your convenience, the total amount of work is' exactly the same when slow cooking or cooking in the standard way. The kinds of recipes that the slow cooker does best are not quick tricks. They are the combination dishes, stews, and medleys that require tasks such as peeling, cutting, and measuring before cooking. With the slow cooker, you can do this preparation when you have the time, and refrigerate the food until cooking time, but your time invested is the same, either way.

But what will matter to you is your own opinion. Base it on experience, not guesswork, by sampling recipes from all the categories. As you get to know your cooker, you'll discover the many ways crock cooking can enhance your own personal cooking style.

CONTENTS

Know Your Cooker 9

    Features of the Slow Cooker 9
    Use and Care 10
      Before You Cook 10
      Play It Safe 10
    Cooking with the Crock 10
      Selecting Recipes 11
      Converting Recipes 11
    Techniques with the Crock 11
      Before the Lid Goes On 11
      During Cooking 12
      After the Lid Comes Off 12

Soups 13

Main Dishes 31

Crockery Cooking: Passport to
International Culinary Adventure 49

    France/Italy 49
      Recipe: Ratatouille 49
    Yugoslavia 50
      Recipe: Sataras 50
    Germany 51
      Recipe: Sauerbraten 51
    Turkey 52
      Recipe: Dolmas 52
    Argentina 53
      Recipe: Carbonada Criolla 53
    Soviet Union 54
      Recipe: Solianka 54
    China/U.S.A. 55

Recipe: Oriental Meat
and Vegetable Stew 55
India/England 56
Recipe: Mulligatawny Soup 56

Meat, Poultry, and Fish 57

Vegetables 71

Breads 79

Desserts 83

Beverages 97

Index 102

KNOW YOUR COOKER

Confused about crocks? No wonder. There are over a baker's (or slow cooker's) dozen, all vying for your favor. Sorting through their many features can lead a shopper to feel that too many cookers can spoil—if not the broth—his power of decision.

What you want is a cooker that offers the most convenience for the price you want to pay. To help you make a choice, here is a rundown of features offered by the slow-cooking pot.

FEATURES OF THE SLOW COOKER

1. It's an electric appliance. It's heated either by coils around the sides or at the base. At least one has a separate pot that lifts off a base somewhat like a hot plate.

The electricity supplies either continuous heat or is controlled by a thermostat. Continuous-heat pots are those that have High, Low, and Off settings. The thermostatically controlled cooker may allow for settings high enough for such jobs as deep-fat frying.

If you want a cooker that will do more than slow-cook, you may prefer the one with the thermostatic switch. The dial is calibrated to show settings up to 500°F. However, the simple High and Low settings can accomplish what the slow cooker does best. That is the lengthy, no-peek variety of cooking that frees the cook for other things when the crock is turned to Low. The Low setting on continuous-heat cookers maintains a temperature of around 180° to 200°F.

The High setting, which keeps the food at a temperature around 300°F, is a convenience feature. It cooks in half the time of the Low setting and helps when you need to speed things up. But it doesn't offer the same "go away and forget it" kind of cooking. Foods with a high sugar content, such as carrots, can get overly brown at this temperature if left too long.

2. Being electric, the slow cooker has a cord. And this becomes a feature, as some pots have detachable cords, while others have permanent ones. If you plan to use your cooker as a serving piece at the table, the permanent cord may be awkward.

3. The slow cooker is usually shaped like a saucepot with either a round or oval opening. The oval pot is a little more adaptable as it can hold such items as whole birds and ham slices that don't conform to the round shape. Capacity ranges from 2½ to 8 quarts.

4. The cooker has a tight-fitting lid which captures the steam that tenderizes those economical cuts of meat. Some lids have a higher dome than others. Height can be an advantage if you use a makeshift cooker insert, such as a coffee can, as some recipes suggest.

5. The "crock" is usually of ceramic stoneware, but some models have liners of glass or metal. Stoneware and glass hold heat better than metal and stand up under normal wear, but they are breakable. The metal ones can withstand greater changes in temperature.

Some crocks are removable from the metal

casings that hold the heating element. These are easier to wash (after cooling to room temperature) and can be used as a separate serving piece.

6. There may be a signal light. It helps, as it prevents leaving a pot turned on inadvertently. Models with thermostatic controls show a light only when the power is on, not when it cycles off. It switches on again when the temperature in the pot drops below the desired level.

USE AND CARE

Packed along with each new slow cooker is a booklet from the manufacturer. The few minutes it takes to read it through may determine how well you'll like your new appliance.

The booklet will tell you what features make your crock unique, and what techniques to use when cooking with it. Most of the instructions are easy; it's changing old habits that's hard. But once you've discovered the flexibility a slow cooker can bring to cooking, you should have plenty of incentive to adjust.

BEFORE YOU COOK

The manufacturer will tell you to wash the crock before using it. If you have a one-piece model, with crock and heating unit combined, you should wash the inside of the pot only.

But if the crock is removable, it can go right into the dishpan. The metal casing should be wiped clean with a damp cloth so that the electric fittings are kept dry.

Cookers with metal pots can be conditioned by rubbing the cooking surface lightly with cooking oil or shortening.

PLAY IT SAFE

The beauty of crock cooking, they say, is that you can "set it and forget it." And it does offer the unique advantage that food will never burn on the Low setting. It will overcook if left too long, but it can be left for a very long time—eighteen hours or more—without harm. This is because steam can't escape; the moisture is captured inside.

But there are precautions you should take to prevent other mishaps with your cooker.

1. Situate the cooker on a moisture-free, level surface so there is no danger of tipping.

2. Keep the pot out of reach of children and pets. You can go away for extended periods, but if you're leaving it, and the children, with a sitter, caution her as you would about food left cooking on the range.

3. If your cooker has a detachable cord, plug it into the appliance with the dial set at Off before plugging it into the outlet. After cooking, set the switch back to Off before unplugging from the outlet. If the heating element is removable, let the base cool before disconnecting it.

4. Place the pot so that the electric cord won't trip anyone. In the kitchen, set the pot at the back of the counter where it won't interfere with your working space. In the dining room, put it on the buffet or some table near an electric outlet, away from paths of traffic. A hot mat under the cooker will protect the surface of the table.

5. Removable crockery pots are made to give long service when kindly treated. But like any ceramic, they are breakable. They shouldn't be used directly on the range top, in the oven, or outdoors. They shouldn't be used to store food in the refrigerator, then transferred directly to the heating element, as sudden temperature changes can crack them. For the same reason, don't put cold water or frozen foods into the ceramic pot when it's hot. And let the crock cool before putting it into the dishwater.

6. Keep the cooker unplugged when not in use. The dial could accidentally be turned on, running up the electric bill and possibly causing a burn.

7. Protect hands with potholders when handling the heated crock. Removing cooker inserts or coffee cans from a hot pot can be a little tricky. In our Test Kitchen, a wooden spatula was used to slip down one side of the insert and pry it up, while the other side was lifted with a potholder.

8. Cords are purposely fairly short on electric slow cookers. That's so they won't dangle and trip you. If possible, locate your cooker close to an outlet. If not, use an extension cord with an electrical rating at least as high as that of the cooker itself. Don't use the extension cord for other appliances while the crock is cooking. If you feel that the cord is heating up, unplug it and make some other arrangement, such as relocating the cooker closer to an outlet.

9. To protect the appearance of teflon-lined metal pots, use utensils with smooth edges to prevent scratching. Don't use steel wool, metal pads, or abrasive scouring powders to clean them. Instead, use a plastic sponge or nylon scouring pad and a thin paste of chlorinated cleanser and water. Scrub gently, then follow up with sudsy water; rinse and dry.

COOKING WITH THE CROCK

Cooking becomes second nature. Once we become accustomed to certain ways, it's not easy to change them. But the advantages of crockery cooking have, for many cooks, proven great enough to make the change worthwhile.

Keep these things in mind as you "re-program" yourself for success with slow cooking.

SELECTING RECIPES

Get acquainted with the types of dishes that the slow cooker does best: soups, stews and other long-cooking meat-and-vegetable combinations, vegetable combos, and fruit medleys. Anything that benefits from steam heat and extended cooking time works beautifully.

This may mean you can now fix recipes you've been avoiding because of long cooking times. It could add a whole new dimension to your meals.

The moist heat also makes ideal conditions to steam puddings. Most cookers can be used for dry baking, too. Some have special baker inserts that you can buy where slow cookers are sold. Or you can use one- or two-pound coffee cans with several layers of paper toweling over the top to absorb moisture. Cakes and quick breads come out deliciously moist, without ever turning on the oven. Come summer, that's a plus you'll appreciate.

Some cooks like to alternate recipes made in the crock, so everything doesn't come out looking like stew. Instead, try cooking a pot roast one day. The next meal from the cooker could be a whole chicken simmered with vegetables. Then, perhaps, fish chowder before you return to those old standbys—the stew variations.

Check the yield of a recipe against the capacity of your cooker. The crock should be at least half full. You can cover less food with foil. If the recipe makes too much for your cooker, cut the recipe.

Check the timing on the recipe to make sure it fits your time schedule for the day. Some people coordinate starting and stopping times with the times they will leave the house and return. Others who feel uncomfortable about leaving the house with an appliance on prefer to dovetail crock cooking with some other all-day project in the house.

CONVERTING RECIPES

After you get the hang of crock cooking, you will probably want to adapt some of your own favorite recipes to use in it. Here are things to keep in mind as you make the conversion.

Fresh milk products do not hold up well in lengthy crock cooking. If the dish needs a creamy look, use evaporated milk or substitute condensed cream soup right from the can. Or wait until the end of the cooking time to add milk, cream, or sour cream.

Pasta and instant rice get mushy when cooked six or eight hours. It's better to cook them separately and stir into the other ingredients near the end of the crock cooking time.

Some seasonings are unpredictable in the pot. Food seems less salty when the salt goes in at the beginning. If you'd like a saltier flavor, put half the salt in at the beginning, and add the rest at the end of the cooking time.

Long cooking develops stronger flavor in many herbs and spices. Try cutting the amount in standard recipes by half. You can always taste and add more later, but it's well-nigh impossible to subtract from flavor once it's there.

Some cooks prefer whole herbs and spices to crushed and ground forms. A whole bay leaf, for example, can be lifted out midway during the cooking time if the flavor is fully developed. It's also possible to tie whole spices in cheesecloth and remove them whenever you like. Through such experimentation, you'll be able to adjust seasonings to your own preference.

Because moisture is captured in the closed cooker, there isn't the evaporation that you expect in other forms of cooking. When converting recipes, try cutting the liquid in half. As with seasonings, more liquid can always be added later if needed.

Cooking time can be cut dramatically by heating the liquid called for in your recipe. Boiling water for soup, then measuring in a heat-proof cup, can reduce cooking length in a recipe that would otherwise take 12 or more hours.

TECHNIQUES WITH THE CROCK

Now for those things that Mother never told you about crock cooking (because there were no electric slow cookers in her day):

BEFORE THE LID GOES ON

1. Browning. For recipes such as stews and pot roast, it helps to brown meat in a skillet, then add to the pot. Some recipes tell you this isn't necessary, but our testing showed that a thorough browning of ten minutes or so produced more attractive and more tender meat.

But if you're looking for shortcuts and don't object to the pale appearance, it's possible to put everything in the pot at once. It does save a little time and cleanup.

2. Vegetables. Crock cooking gives different results with vegetables than standard cooking. In some types of crocks, vegetables take longer than the meat to reach tenderness. Experiment with your cooker; layering vegetables at the bottom of the pot may facilitate cooking.

3. Thickening. Recipes can be thickened at the beginning by stirring in three or four tablespoons of tapioca. Other ways are suggested in the next section on "After the Lid Comes Off."

4. Setting the control. Some recipes offer a choice of Low or High settings; others may indicate only one. But timing for High settings can be converted to Low by doubling the time length. And Low settings can convert to High by doing the reverse: cut time in half. Your choice will depend on the time available to you.

Low gives the tenderness and pleasant mingling of flavors for which crock cooking is famous. Cooking on High is more like standard cooking, but offers a handy shortcut when one is needed. It is advisable to stir occasionally when cooking on High.

DURING COOKING

The directions for cooking at the Low setting could be the easiest ever given: Do nothing. Peeking only lets out steam, and that means adding 15 to 20 minutes to the cooking time for it to build up again.

On the High setting, as mentioned, an occasional stir may be needed to prevent certain foods from sticking. And some recipes call for the addition of ingredients before the end of the cooking time. These are ingredients such as fish, mushrooms, or pasta, which cook in less time than the other recipe components.

AFTER THE LID COMES OFF

Most crock recipes give a range of cooking time such as "6 to 8 hours." Check at the end of the minimum time to see if the food is done to your liking. If it isn't tender, give it more time. If you're running late, turn a cooker that has been on Low up to High. That will cut remaining time in half.

On the other hand, if the meat is done in six hours and you'd planned dinner for a later hour, turn the cooker off and let the dish "rest" until serving time, rather than let the food overcook.

After cooking is the time to add those foods that cannot go in at the beginning: sour cream, cooked pasta, and the like. Stir them in just to heat through before serving.

If the sauce needs more thickening, take your choice of these methods:

1. Mix one tablespoon of flour or cornstarch for each cup of cooking liquid with enough cold water to make a smooth paste. Stir into the pot liquid and turn the heat up to high. With the lid off, stir the sauce until it reaches the thickness you like.

2. Taking a leaf from the French chef, mix equal parts of butter or margarine and flour. One tablespoon of this mixture will thicken a cup of pot liquid.

RECIPE CONVERSION TIME CHART

If original recipe calls for:	cook on Low for:	cook on High for:
$1/4$ to $1/2$ hour	4 to 8 hours	$1^{1}/_{2}$ to $2^{1}/_{2}$ hours
$1/2$ to 1 hour	6 to 8 hours	3 to 4 hours
1 to 3 hours	8 to 16 hours	4 to 6 hours

SOUPS

Soup of the evening, beautiful soup!

LEWIS CARROLL

Beef Stock

- 2 large onions, peeled
- 2 whole cloves
- 2 pounds lean beef chuck or plate, cut in 1-inch pieces
- 1 soup bone, cracked
- 5 carrots, pared and cut in large pieces
- 2 white turnips, pared and cut in large pieces
- 3 stalks celery with leaves, sliced
- 4 leeks, washed and sliced
- 3 sprigs parsley
- 1½ tablespoons salt
- ¼ teaspoon thyme
- 3 quarts cold water

1. Slice 1 onion; put cloves into the other onion.
2. Put beef, soup bone, onions, carrots, and remaining ingredients into an electric cooker.
3. Cover and cook on High 1 hour. Turn cooker control to Low and cook 10 to 12 hours.
4. Remove soup bone and strain stock. Cool stock and skim fat.
5. Store stock in a covered·container in refrigerator.

2 quarts stock

Hot Borsch with Beef

- 2 cans (16 ounces each) whole beets, drained (reserve liquid)
- 1 pound lean beef (chuck or plate)
- 1 small soup bone, cracked
- 2 small onions, peeled
- 1½ teaspoons salt
- ⅛ teaspoon pepper
- 3½ cups water
- 2 tablespoons lemon juice
- 1 teaspoon sugar

1. Cut the beets into fine strips; set aside.
2. Put the beef and soup bone into an electric cooker. Add the reserved beet liquid, the beet strips, onions, salt, pepper, and water.
3. Cover and cook on Low 10 to 12 hours.
4. Remove the meat and soup bone. Cut meat into slices.
5. Just before serving, ·blend lemon juice and sugar into soup and ladle into bowls. Serve meat slices separately.

About 1½ quarts soup

Cabbage Soup

- 1 pound beef shank cross cuts
- 2 or 3 marrow bones
- 1 cup chopped onion
- 2 quarts water
- 1 small head cabbage, shredded
- 3 tablespoons salt
- 3 tablespoons sugar
- ½ cup lemon juice
- 1 tablespoon fat
- 2 tablespoons flour
- Snipped parsley

1. Put meat, bones, onion, and water into a large electric cooker.
2. Cover and cook on Low 10 to 12 hours.
3. Sprinkle cabbage with salt and let stand 1 to 2 hours. Pour boiling water over cabbage and drain thoroughly.
4. Remove bones and cut meat into small pieces; return meat to soup. Add drained cabbage; stir.
5. Cover and cook on High 1 hour.
6. Stir in sugar and lemon juice.
7. Melt fat in a skillet; add flour. Stir over medium heat until flour becomes a deep brown. Gradually add some of the soup, stirring until smooth. Slowly pour flour mixture into soup, stirring constantly to prevent lumping.
8. Add more salt or sugar to taste, if desired. Pour into individual serving bowls; sprinkle with parsley.

About 3 quarts soup

Norwegian Vegetable Soup with Beef

- 3 pounds beef short ribs
- 1 small head cabbage, cut in pieces
- 2 medium onions, peeled and chopped
- 2 medium carrots, pared and chopped
- 1 whole nutmeg
- 2 beef bouillon cubes
- 2 teaspoons salt
- ¼ teaspoon pepper
- 2 quarts boiling water
- ½ cup finely chopped parsley
  Horseradish Sauce (see below)

1. Put short ribs into an electric cooker with cabbage, onion, carrot, nutmeg, bouillon cubes, salt, pepper, and water.
2. Cover and cook on Low 8 to 10 hours, or until vegetables are tender and meat is done.
3. Remove meat to serving dish and keep warm.
4. Measure 2 cups of broth from soup to make horseradish sauce for meat. Stir parsley into remaining soup. Serve soup, then meat with horseradish sauce.

About 2 quarts soup

Horseradish Sauce: Heat **¼ cup butter or margarine** in a saucepan over low heat. Blend in **¼ cup flour, 4 teaspoons sugar,** and **¼ teaspoon salt.** Stir until mixture bubbles. Remove from heat and gradually add reserved soup broth from recipe above. Add **2 tablespoons** each **vinegar** and **prepared horseradish.** Cook until sauce thickens.

Ham-Vegetable Soup

- 1 meaty ham bone
- 2 cups diced potatoes
- 1 cup diced carrots
- ½ cup chopped celery
- 1 small onion, peeled and sliced
- ½ teaspoon salt
- ⅛ teaspoon pepper
- 1½ quarts hot water

1. Combine all ingredients in an electric cooker.
2. Cover and cook on Low 6 to 8 hours.

About 2 quarts soup

Beef Encore Soup

A delicious use for leftover beef roast.

- 2 to 3 cups chopped cooked beef roast
- 3 stalks celery, chopped
- 2 carrots, pared and sliced
- 2 small onions, peeled and chopped
- 1 can (16 ounces) tomatoes (undrained)
- 1 package (10 ounces) frozen mixed vegetables
- 1 package (1⅝ ounces) chili seasoning mix
- 1½ quarts water
- ⅓ cup butter, melted
- ½ cup flour

1. Combine all ingredients except butter and flour in an electric cooker.
2. Cover and cook on Low 8 to 10 hours.
3. One hour before serving, turn cooker control to High. Blend butter and flour until smooth. Pour into soup, stirring constantly until mixture is well blended. Cook and stir until soup is thickened.

4 to 6 servings

Dutch Vegetable Soup

- 1 large soup bone
- 1 can (16 ounces) tomatoes (undrained), or 2 cups chopped tomatoes
- 1 can (16 ounces) lima beans (undrained)
- 1 can (16 ounces) whole kernel corn (undrained)
- 1 large turnip, pared and finely diced
- 1 carrot, pared and sliced
- 1 onion, peeled and sliced
- 2 teaspoons salt
- ¼ teaspoon pepper
- 2 quarts boiling water
- 1 tablespoon flour
- ½ cup milk

1. Combine all ingredients except flour and milk in electric cooker.
2. Cover and cook on Low 8 to 10 hours, or until vegetables are tender.
3. Add a little milk to flour to make a paste; add remaining milk and stir until smooth. Add to cooker; stir.
4. Cook on High 15 to 30 minutes, stirring occasionally, until thickened. Serve hot.

About 3 quarts soup

Vegetable-Beef Soup

- 1 beef soup bone, cracked
- 2 pounds beef for stew
- 4 uncooked chicken pieces (neck, back, and wings)
- 1 teaspoon salt
  Few grains black pepper
- 1 small clove garlic, peeled and minced
- 6 tablespoons regular barley
- 3 large carrots, pared and cut in ½-inch dice
- 2 medium potatoes, pared and cut in ½-inch dice
- 2 or 3 stalks celery, cut in ½-inch dice
- 1 turnip, pared and cut in ½-inch dice
- ½ cup fresh green peas or cut green beans
- 3 quarts water
- 1 quart canned tomatoes, drained
- 1 cup chopped raw cabbage
- ½ cup canned corn, drained
- 2 tablespoons prepared gravy seasoning or 2 teaspoons Worcestershire sauce
- ½ teaspoon celery salt
- ½ teaspoon onion salt
- ¼ teaspoon garlic salt

1. Put beef bone, meat, and chicken in a large electric cooker. Add salt, pepper, garlic, barley, carrots, potatoes, celery, turnip, peas, and water.
2. Cover and cook on Low 10 to 12 hours.
3. Remove bones from soup. Add remaining vegetables and seasonings to cooker; mix.
4. Cover and cook on High 30 to 45 minutes.

About 4 quarts soup

Oxtail Soup

- 1 oxtail (about 3 pounds), disjointed
- 2 medium onions, peeled and sliced
- 2 large carrots, pared and sliced
- 2 potatoes, pared and cut in ½-inch cubes
- 2 stalks celery with leaves, sliced diagonally
- 2 fresh tomatoes, peeled and sliced, or 1 can (8 ounces) tomatoes
- ¼ cup regular barley
- 1 package (2⅝ ounces) oxtail soup mix
- 2 quarts water

1. Put oxtail pieces on rack of broiler pan and brown under broiler, turning as necessary.
2. Transfer oxtail to an electric cooker. Add remaining ingredients; stir.
3. Cover and cook on Low 8 to 10 hours.

About 3 quarts soup

Oxtail Soup Paprikash

- 1 oxtail (about 2 pounds), cut in pieces
- ¼ cup flour
  Salt and pepper
- 2 tablespoons fat
- 2 quarts hot water
- 2 green peppers, seeded and cut in thin strips
- 4 onions, peeled and finely sliced
- 2 cloves garlic, finely minced
- 1 tablespoon paprika
  Freshly ground pepper
- 1 pint dairy sour cream

1. Dredge the oxtail pieces in flour mixed with salt and pepper. Brown thoroughly in hot fat. Transfer meat to an electric cooker.
2. Add part of the water to skillet and stir while heating to release all the meaty particles.
3. Add remaining ingredients, except sour cream, to cooker, then add liquid from skillet and remaining water.
4. Cover and cook on Low 8 to 10 hours, or until meat is quite tender.
5. Serve soup with sour cream in a separate bowl.

About 8 servings

Vegetable Soup, Minestrone Style

- **2 tablespoons vegetable oil**
- **2 pounds beef for stew (1-inch pieces)**
- **1 cup chopped celery**
- **¾ cup chopped onion**
- **2 tablespoons chopped parsley**
- **1 clove garlic, minced**
- **1 tablespoon salt**
- **¼ teaspoon pepper**
- **½ teaspoon oregano, crushed**
- **2 cans (8 ounces each) tomato sauce**
- **1 quart water**
- **1 cup broken spaghetti**
- **1½ cups sliced zucchini**
- **1 package (10 ounces) frozen peas, partially thawed**

1. Heat oil in a large skillet. Add meat and brown on all sides. Push meat to the side; put celery, onion, parsley, and garlic into fat and cook until celery is tender. Add seasonings and tomato sauce; stir to mix contents of skillet. Turn mixture into an electric cooker. Add water and stir.
2. Cover and cook on Low 8 to 10 hours.
3. Add spaghetti, zucchini, and peas; stir.
4. Cover and cook on High 30 to 45 minutes.

10 to 12 servings

Escarole Soup

- **3 pounds beef shank cross cuts**
- **1 can (6 ounces) tomato paste**
- **1 tablespoon salt**
- **1 teaspoon basil, crushed**
- **½ teaspoon oregano, crushed**
- **2 quarts water**
- **1 medium onion, peeled and diced**
- **1 medium potato, pared and diced**
- **2 stalks celery, diced**
- **1 pound escarole, chopped**

1. Put beef into an electric cooker. Add tomato paste, salt, basil, oregano, and water; stir.
2. Cover and cook on Low 10 to 16 hours.
3. Remove meat from liquid; discard bones. Return meat to cooker and add onion, potato, and celery; stir.
4. Cover and cook on High 30 minutes.
5. Add escarole to cooker; stir.
6. Cover and cook on High 30 minutes.
7. Serve soup garnished with **snipped parsley** and **freshly ground black pepper**.

About 3 quarts soup

Sausage Soup Italiano

- **1½ to 2 pounds mild Italian sausage, cut in pieces**
- **2 onions, peeled and chopped**
- **2 cloves garlic, minced**
- **1 can (28 ounces) Italian-style tomatoes (undrained)**
- **2 medium zucchini, sliced**
- **1 large green pepper, seeded and chopped**
- **2 quarts beef broth (homemade, canned, or made using bouillon cubes)**
- **1 cup dry red wine, such as chianti**
- **1 package (3 ounces) spaghetti sauce mix with mushrooms**
- **1 package (7 ounces) elbow macaroni**
  Grated Parmesan cheese

1. Brown sausage; remove from skillet and reserve.
2. Sauté onion and garlic in sausage fat until tender.
3. Combine sausage, onion, garlic, and vegetables in an electric cooker. Add beef broth and wine.
4. Add enough cold water to the spaghetti sauce mix to make a smooth paste. Stir it into the mixture in cooker until well blended.
5. Cover and cook on Low 6 to 8 hours, or until vegetables are tender.
6. Near the end of cooking period, cook macaroni according to package directions and stir into soup in cooker. Serve with Parmesan cheese.

About 8 servings

Soup with Meatballs

Broth:
- 1 quart beef broth (homemade, canned, or from bouillon cubes)
- 1 quart sieved canned tomatoes
- ¼ cup minced onion
- 1 teaspoon chili powder
- 1 teaspoon salt
- ½ teaspoon pepper
- 1 sprig mint

Meatballs:
- ⅓ cup fine dry bread crumbs
- ¼ cup water
- ¼ pound ground beef
- ¼ pound ground pork
- 1 egg, beaten
- 2 teaspoons minced onion
- 1 teaspoon lemon juice
- ½ teaspoon chili powder
- ½ teaspoon salt
- ¼ teaspoon thyme
- 1 tablespoon fat

1. Put all ingredients for broth into an electric cooker.
2. Cover and cook on High while preparing meatballs.
3. For meatballs, combine bread crumbs and water; set aside. Put meat, egg, onion, and lemon juice into a bowl, sprinkle with dry seasonings, and mix lightly with a fork. Blend in bread crumb mixture. Shape into balls about ¾ inch in diameter.
4. Heat fat in a skillet, add meatballs, and brown on all sides.
5. Remove mint from broth and add meatballs.
6. Cover and cook on Low 6 to 8 hours.

About 8 servings

Turkey-Lentil Soup

- 1 turkey carcass, broken into pieces
- 1 cup dried lentils, rinsed
- 2 onions, peeled and sliced
- 2 carrots, pared and thinly sliced
- 2 stalks celery with leaves, sliced
- 1 tablespoon salt
- Water

1. Put as much of the turkey carcass into an electric cooker as will fit with the lid on. If using a small cooker, use chunks of turkey cut off the bones, or chicken parts.
2. Add lentils, vegetables, salt, and water to within 1 inch of top edge of cooker.
3. Cover and cook on Low 8 to 10 hours.
4. Remove turkey carcass from pot. Remove any meat from bones and return to soup.

About 8 servings

As you get to know your cooker, you'll discover the many ways crock cooking can enhance your own cooking style.

Soup Mexicana

- 1 chicken breast
- 1½ quarts chicken broth (homemade or made from bouillon cubes)
- 2 onions, peeled and chopped
- 2 cups chopped zucchini
- 1 cup drained canned whole kernel corn
- ⅓ cup tomato purée
- 2 ounces cream cheese, cut in small cubes
- 2 avocados, peeled and sliced

1. Put chicken breast into an electric cooker; add broth and onion.
2. Cover and cook on Low 6 to 8 hours.
3. Remove chicken; dice meat and return to broth. Add zucchini, corn, and tomato purée; mix.
4. Cover and cook on High 30 minutes.
5. Just before serving, mix in cream cheese and avocado.

6 to 8 servings

Country-Style Chicken Soup

- 1 chicken (about 3 pounds), cut in pieces
- 6 chicken bouillon cubes
- 1 teaspoon seasoned salt
- 2 large onions, cut in pieces, or 6 tiny whole white onions
- 6 carrots, pared and sliced diagonally, or 12 tiny whole carrots
- 6 stalks celery with tops, sliced diagonally
- 1 bay leaf
- 1½ quarts water
- 2 cans (8 ounces each) or 1 can (15 ounces) tomato sauce
- ½ cup chopped parsley
- 1 can (about 8 ounces) whole kernel corn, drained

1. Put chicken pieces into an electric cooker. Add bouillon cubes, seasoned salt, onion, carrot, celery, bay leaf, and water.
2. Cover and cook on Low 10 to 12 hours.
3. Remove bay leaf and chicken from cooker. Separate chicken meat from skin and bones. Return meat to cooker with tomato sauce, parsley, and corn; mix.
4. Cover and cook on High 30 minutes.

About 6 servings

Chicken-Vegetable Soup

- 3 pounds chicken pieces (breasts, legs, thighs, and wings)
- 4 cups cut celery (2-inch pieces)
- 2 small onions, peeled and finely chopped
- 2 tablespoons salt
- ⅛ teaspoon rosemary
- 3 quarts hot water
- 1 cup defrosted frozen green peas

1. Put all ingredients, except peas, into an electric cooker.
2. Cover and cook on High until mixture boils, about 2 hours. Turn cooker control to Low and cook 4 hours.
3. Remove chicken pieces from soup and separate meat from bones and skin. Return meat to soup, add peas, and stir.
4. Cover and cook on Low 30 minutes.

About 3½ quarts soup

Chicken-Corn Soup

- 5 pounds chicken pieces
- 1 stalk celery with leaves, cut in pieces
- 1 onion, peeled and cut in quarters
- 1 tablespoon salt
- ¼ teaspoon saffron
- 2 quarts cold water
- 3 cups corn kernels (fresh, frozen, or canned)
- 2 cups uncooked egg noodles
- ⅛ teaspoon pepper

1. Put chicken pieces into an electric cooker. Add celery, onion, salt, saffron, and water.
2. Cover and cook on High 1 hour. Turn cooker control to Low and cook 18 to 22 hours.
3. Remove chicken. Strain broth and skim off fat. Return broth to cooker. Discard chicken skin and bones; cut meat into pieces and add to broth. Add corn, noodles, and pepper; stir.
4. Cover and cook on High 20 to 30 minutes, or until noodles are tender.
5. Serve soup garnished with **snipped parsley** and **chopped hard-cooked egg.**

About 3 quarts soup

Chicken-Noodle Soup

- 1 chicken (about 3 pounds), cut in pieces
- 2 stalks celery, chopped
- 1 onion, peeled and chopped
- 1 carrot, pared and chopped
- ¼ cup chopped parsley
- 1 tablespoon salt
- ½ teaspoon basil
- ¼ teaspoon pepper
- 1 bay leaf
- 2 quarts water
- 1 package (8 ounces) egg noodles

1. Put all ingredients, except noodles, into an electric cooker.
2. Cover and cook on Low 5 to 6 hours.
3. Remove chicken and bay leaf. Discard chicken skin and bones; dice meat and return to broth. Add noodles; stir.
4. Cover and cook on Low 1 hour, or until noodles are done.

About 6 servings

Creamy Creole Gumbo

  2 tablespoons butter or margarine
  ½ cup thinly sliced onion
  ¼ cup chopped green pepper
  2 tablespoons flour
  1 teaspoon salt
  ¼ teaspoon pepper
  ½ teaspoon leaf thyme
    Few drops Tabasco
  1 can (7½ ounces) crab meat, drained
  1 cup canned okra with liquid
  1 can (16 ounces) tomatoes (undrained)
  2 cups milk

1. Heat butter in a saucepan. Add onion and green pepper; cook until tender. Stir in flour and seasonings; heat until bubbly.
2. Turn contents of saucepan into an electric cooker. Add Tabasco, crab meat, okra, and tomatoes; mix.
3. Cover and cook on Low 1 hour.
4. Add milk to cooker; mix.
5. Cover and cook on Low 1 hour.

About 1½ quarts soup

Gumbo Filé

  1 stewing chicken (4 to 5 pounds), cut in
    pieces
  2 teaspoons salt
  1 small onion
  3 sprigs parsley
  2 pieces celery with leaves
  1 bay leaf
  2 or 3 peppercorns
  2 quarts water
  1 pint oysters
  2 tablespoons butter or margarine
  2 medium onions, peeled and chopped
  ½ pound cooked ham, cut in ½-inch pieces
  ⅛ teaspoon each black pepper, cayenne
    pepper, and chili powder
  2 tablespoons filé powder

1. Put chicken into a large electric cooker. Add salt, onion, parsley, celery, bay leaf, peppercorns, and water.
2. Cover and cook on Low 10 to 12 hours.
3. Remove chicken from broth. Strain broth and cool slightly. Remove fat which rises to surface. Return 3 cups broth to cooker. Cool chicken slightly and remove skin and bones; dice chicken and add to broth in cooker.
4. Drain oysters, reserving liquor. Pick over oysters and remove shell particles. Set aside.
5. Heat butter in a skillet over low heat. Add chopped onion and ham; cook until onion is soft. Add contents of skillet to cooker; add oysters, reserved oyster liquor, peppers, and chili powder; stir.
6. Cover and cook on Low 1 hour, or until edges of oysters begin to curl.
7. Unplug cooker. Mix about ½ cup liquid with the filé powder. Thoroughly blend with mixture in cooker.
8. Serve gumbo over mounds of **fluffy cooked rice.**

About 8 servings

Note: Filé powder should always be added after the gumbo has been removed from the heat. If filé powder is cooked, the gumbo will become stringy and unpalatable.

Red Snapper Soup

  1 red snapper (1½ to 2 pounds)
    White Wine Court Bouillon (see below)
    Special Brown Sauce (see below)
  ½ cup diced green pepper
  ¼ cup diced onion
  ¼ cup diced celery
  ¼ cup dry sherry

1. Remove head, skin, bones, fins, and tail from red snapper; reserve meat in refrigerator.
2. Prepare court bouillon in an electric cooker. Add onion, celery, and green pepper to court bouillon.

3. Cover and cook on Low 4 hours, or until vegetables are tender.

4. Prepare brown sauce during the last half-hour of cooking time for vegetables. Slowly add the brown sauce to vegetable mixture; blend thoroughly. Add reserved red snapper meat.

5. Cook on High until fish is tender, about 30 minutes.

About 2 quarts soup

White Wine Court Bouillon: In an electric cooker, combine fish trimmings, **1 quart boiling water, 1 cup dry white wine, 1 medium onion, quartered, 1 medium carrot, sliced, 2 slices lemon, 3 whole cloves, 3 whole peppercorns, celery tops, 1 sprig parsley, 1 bay leaf, 1 teaspoon salt,** and **1 pinch each celery seed, thyme,** and **marjoram.** Cover and cook on Low 4 hours. Strain stock and return to cooker.

Special Brown Sauce: Brown **¼ cup flour** in **¼ cup butter or margarine.** Gradually stir in **2 cups chicken stock** (homemade, canned, or from bouillon cubes) and **2 cans (6 ounces each) tomato paste.** Simmer slowly, stirring occasionally.

Pacific Seafood Chowder

   3 **medium potatoes, pared and cut in ½-inch pieces**
   1 **large sweet Spanish onion, peeled and thinly sliced**
  ¾ **cup chopped celery**
  ¼ **cup chopped green pepper**
   2 **cloves garlic, minced**
1½ **teaspoons salt**
  ¼ **teaspoon pepper**
  ¼ **teaspoon thyme**
  ¼ **teaspoon marjoram**
   2 **cups clam-tomato juice**
1½ **pounds North Pacific halibut, fresh or frozen**
   1 **can (7½ ounces) Alaska King crab or 1 package (6 ounces) frozen Alaska King crab**
   1 **dozen small hard-shell clams**
   2 **cans (16 ounces each) tomatoes (undrained) Snipped parsley**

1. Layer vegetables and seasonings in an electric cooker. Pour clam-tomato juice over all.
2. Cover and cook on Low 4 to 6 hours.
3. Defrost halibut, if frozen. Cut into 1-inch chunks. Drain canned crab and slice. Or defrost, drain, and slice frozen crab.
4. Add seafood and tomatoes with liquid.
5. Cover and cook on High 1 to 2 hours.
6. Sprinkle with parsley. Serve with **buttered crusty bread.**

About 8 servings

Macaroni-Tuna Soup

  ¼ **cup butter or margarine**
   1 **medium onion, peeled and chopped**
   1 **cup diced celery**
   1 **teaspoon salt**
  ¾ **teaspoon bouquet garni for soup Few grains cayenne pepper**
   1 **quart chicken broth**
   1 **cup uncooked elbow macaroni**
   2 **cans (6½ or 7 ounces each) tuna, drained and flaked**
   1 **can (3 ounces) chopped broiled mushrooms (undrained)**
   2 **cups half-and-half, heated**

1. Heat butter in saucepan and add onion; sauté.
2. Put the onion, celery, salt, bouquet garni, cayenne pepper, and broth into an electric cooker.
3. Cover and cook on Low 4 to 6 hours.
4. Add macaroni to cooker along with tuna, mushrooms, and half-and-half.
5. Cover and cook on Low 1 hour.

8 to 10 servings

Salmon Chowder

    3   tablespoons butter
    ½   cup chopped onion
    2   tablespoons chopped green pepper
    1   can (about 10 ounces) condensed cream of
        celery soup
    3   cups milk
    1½ cups diced pared potatoes, cooked
    1   cup diced pared carrots, cooked
    1   can (16 ounces) tomatoes, drained
    1   teaspoon salt
    ¼   teaspoon pepper
    1   can (16 ounces) pink salmon, drained, skin
        and bones discarded, and meat separated
        in chunks

1. Heat butter in a large saucepan. Add onion and green pepper; cook until tender.
2. Turn contents of saucepan into an electric cooker. Add soup, milk, potatoes, carrots, tomatoes, salt, pepper, and salmon; mix.
3. Cover and cook on Low 2 hours.

8 to 10 servings

> **T**he beauty of crock cooking, they say, is that you can "set it and forget it."

Bean Soup

    7   cups water
    1   pound dried navy beans, rinsed
    3   medium potatoes, pared
    3   medium onions, peeled
    2   stalks celery
    3   sprigs parsley
    1   clove garlic, peeled
    1   large meaty ham bone
    1   teaspoon salt
    ½   teaspoon pepper
    5   cups water

1. Bring 7 cups water to boiling in a saucepot or Dutch oven. Add beans, bring to boiling, and boil 2 minutes. Remove from heat; cover and let stand 1 hour.
2. Finely chop potatoes, onions, celery, parsley, and garlic.
3. Turn beans and water into a large electric cooker. Add ham bone, seasonings, and finely chopped ingredients.
4. Cover and cook on Low 10 to 12 hours.
5. Remove bone from soup. Remove any meat from bone, cut into small pieces, and mix with soup.

8 to 10 servings

Black Bean Soup

    1   pound dried black beans, rinsed
    1   ham bone or ¼ pound salt pork
    1   cup diced carrot
    ½   cup diced celery
    ½   cup diced onion
    2   teaspoons salt
        Few grains cayenne pepper
    ¼   cup melted butter
    2   quarts water
    1   tablespoon lemon juice
    1   cup milk
    ¼   cup sherry (optional)

1. Put beans into a large saucepan. Add 1½ quarts water. Cover and let stand overnight.
2. The next day, drain beans and put into an

electric cooker. Add ham bone, diced vegetables. salt, cayenne, butter, and water; mix.

3. Cover and cook on Low 8 to 10 hours.

4. Remove ham bone. Drain vegetables, reserving liquid. Put vegetables through a food mill. Return purée and liquid to cooker. Stir in lemon juice, then milk.

5. Cover and cook on Low 1 hour.

6. Just before serving, mix in sherry (if using). Serve topped with **croutons** or diced cooked salt pork (if used).

About 2 quarts soup

cooker. Add celery, onion, pimento, salt, and pepper; stir.

3. Cover and cook on Low 6 to 8 hours.

4. Strain liquid and return to cooker. Force vegetables through a food mill into broth. Stir in bouillon.

5. Put sour cream into a bowl; add 1 cup broth gradually, stirring constantly. Blend into remaining soup.

6. Cover and cook on Low 1 hour.

About 1 quart soup

Greek Bean Soup

  2 quarts water
  1 pound dried navy beans, rinsed
  ½ cup olive oil
  1 can (16 ounces) tomatoes (undrained)
  4 stalks celery with leaves, chopped
  1 large onion, peeled and finely chopped
  2 carrots, pared and thinly sliced
  2 teaspoons salt
  ¼ teaspoon pepper
  2 quarts water

1. Bring 2 quarts water to boiling in a saucepot or Dutch oven. Add beans, bring to boiling, and boil 2 minutes. Remove from heat; cover and let stand 1 hour.

2. Turn beans and liquid into a large electric cooker; add remaining ingredients and stir well.

3. Cover and cook on Low 10 to 12 hours, or until beans are very soft.

8 to 10 servings

Lima Bean Bisque

  1 quart water
  ½ pound dried large lima beans, rinsed
  1 stalk celery, finely chopped
  1 onion, peeled and chopped
  1 pimento, minced
  1 teaspoon salt
  ⅛ teaspoon white pepper
  2 teaspoons instant beef bouillon
  1 cup dairy sour cream

1. Bring water to boiling in a saucepan. Add beans, bring to boiling, and boil 2 minutes. Remove from heat; cover and let stand 1 hour.

2. Turn contents of saucepan into an electric

Bean, Barley, and Sausage Soup

  1 pound dried kidney beans, rinsed
  1 cup regular barley
  12 ounces smoked Polish sausage, cut in pieces
  2 cloves garlic, peeled
  1 tablespoon salt
  Parsley sprigs
  1½ to 2 quarts water

1. Put beans into a large saucepan. Add 1½ quarts water. Cover and let stand overnight.

2. The next day, drain off water. Put beans, barley, and remaining ingredients into an electric cooker; stir.

3. Cover and cook on High 4 hours.

6 to 8 servings

Split Pea Soup

        1 pound dried split peas, rinsed
     1½ pounds smoked ham hocks
        1 cup chopped onion
        ½ cup sliced celery
        2 teaspoons salt
        6 whole peppercorns
        1 bay leaf
     1½ quarts water

1. Put all ingredients into an electric cooker.
2. Cover and cook on Low 8 to 10 hours.
3. Remove ham hocks and dice meat; reserve ham. Discard bay leaf and peppercorns.
4. Pour soup, about one quarter at a time, into an electric blender and blend until smooth. Return soup to cooker, mix in ham, and keep hot until serving time.

6 to 8 servings

Timing for High settings can be converted to Low by doubling the time length. Low settings can convert to High by cutting time in half.

Blender Pea Soup

        1 can (17 ounces) green peas (undrained)
     1½ cups milk
        2 tablespoons butter or margarine
        2 teaspoons flour
        ½ teaspoon salt
        ½ teaspoon nutmeg
        ¼ teaspoon sugar
        1 small onion, peeled and quartered

1. Put peas with liquid into an electric blender container. Add 1 cup milk, butter, flour, salt, nutmeg, and sugar. Cover and blend thoroughly. Remove cover and add onion, a quarter at a time, continuing to blend.
2. Pour mixture into an electric cooker.
3. Use the remaining ½ cup milk to rinse out blender (cover blender and turn on, then off). Pour into cooker.
4. Cover and cook on Low 1 hour.

About 1 quart soup

Split Pea-Vegetable Soup

        1 pound dried green split peas, rinsed
        4 leeks, washed thoroughly and cut in large pieces
        2 large onions, peeled and cut in large pieces
        1 bunch green onions, diced
        4 large carrots, pared and diced
        2 teaspoons salt
        ⅛ teaspoon pepper
        4 quarts water
        ¼ cup butter or margarine
        ½ pound fresh mushrooms, cleaned and diced
        1 package (10 ounces) frozen cut okra, defrosted
        1 package (10 ounces) frozen whole kernel corn, defrosted
        2 cans (about 10 ounces each) condensed beef broth
        2 cans (about 13 ounces each) chicken broth

1. Put split peas into a large electric cooker. Add leek, onion, carrot, salt, pepper, and water; mix.
2. Cover and cook on Low 4 hours.
3. Heat butter in a skillet. Add mushrooms and cook until lightly browned.
4. Add browned mushrooms, okra, corn, and broth to split pea mixture; stir.
5. Cover and cook on Low 2 hours.
6. Serve garnished with **dairy sour cream** and **snipped parsley.**

About 4 quarts soup

Garbanzo Bean-Salami Soup

        1 meaty ham bone
        1 medium onion, coarsely chopped
        1 clove garlic, crushed or minced
        2 cups diced potato
        1 teaspoon salt
        ¼ teaspoon black pepper
        ⅛ teaspoon powdered saffron
        3 quarts water
        4 ounces salami, cut in pieces
        1 can (15½ ounces) chickpeas (garbanzos), drained

1. Put ham bone, onion, garlic, potato, seasonings, and water into a large electric cooker.

2. Cover and cook on Low 8 to 10 hours.
3. Remove ham bone from broth. Remove meat from bone; dice meat and return to cooker. Stir in salami and chickpeas.
4. Cover and cook on Low 30 minutes.

About 3½ quarts soup

Lentil Soup with Frankfurters

1½ cups (about ½ pound) dried lentils, rinsed
  1 ham bone, cracked
  2 stalks celery, sliced
  2 carrots, pared or scraped and sliced
  1 teaspoon salt
  ¼ teaspoon pepper
  3 sprigs chervil or parsley
  2 quarts beef broth (homemade or made from bouillon cubes)
  2 tablespoons butter
  2 medium onions, peeled and thinly sliced
  6 frankfurters, cut diagonally in ½-inch slices

1. Put lentils, ham bone, celery, carrot, seasonings, and broth into an electric cooker.
2. Cover and cook on Low 8 to 10 hours.
3. Remove ham bone. Force soup mixture through a food mill and return to cooker.

4. Heat butter in a skillet. Add onions and frankfurters. Cook until onion is tender and frank slices are lightly browned. Add to soup; mix.
5. Cover and cook on High 20 to 30 minutes.

About 2 quarts soup

Soup Kettle Supper

  4 ounces sliced bacon, cut in pieces
  2 cups diced cooked ham
  1 can (about 10 ounces) condensed beef broth
  2 cups water
1⅓ cups packaged precooked rice
  1 can (17 ounces) whole kernel corn (undrained)
  1 can (16 ounces) green beans (undrained)
  1 can (16 ounces) tomatoes (undrained)
  1 teaspoon salt
  ⅛ teaspoon pepper

1. Fry bacon in a kettle or Dutch oven until done. Remove bacon and drain on absorbent paper.
2. Pour off all but 2 tablespoons of the drippings. Fry ham in the hot bacon drippings in kettle until slightly browned.
3. Put ham, bacon, and remaining ingredients into an electric cooker.
4. Cover and cook on High 2 hours.
5. Sprinkle soup with **snipped parsley** and serve.

About 8 servings

Yellow Pea Soup with Pork

  ¾ pound (about 1⅔ cups) dried yellow peas, rinsed
  1 pound smoked pork shoulder roll
  ¾ cup coarsely chopped onion
  1 teaspoon salt
  ¼ teaspoon sugar
  1 teaspoon leaf thyme
  3 quarts water

1. Cover peas with 2½ quarts water in a large saucepan; cover and let stand overnight.
2. The next day, drain peas and put into an electric cooker. Add smoked pork, onion, seasonings, and 3 quarts water.
3. Cover and cook on Low 10 to 12 hours.
4. Remove meat. Skim fat from soup.
5. Serve soup with thin slices of the smoked pork.

About 2½ quarts soup

Creamy Carrot Soup

¼ cup butter or margarine
¼ to ½ cup chopped onion
2 cups thinly sliced carrots (about 1 pound)
½ teaspoon salt
3 cups hot chicken broth (homemade, canned, or from bouillon cubes)
¼ cup uncooked rice
2 cups half-and-half

1. Heat butter in a large skillet. Add onion and cook until lightly browned. Add carrots, sprinkle with salt, and toss until carrots are coated. Cook, tightly covered, over low heat 20 minutes, stirring occasionally.
2. Turn contents of skillet into an electric cooker. Add broth and rice; stir.
3. Cover and cook on Low 4 to 6 hours.
4. Pour soup, a portion at a time, into an electric blender; blend until smooth. Return soup to cooker and add half-and-half; stir.
5. Cover and cook on Low 1 hour.
6. Garnish soup with **snipped chives, parsley,** or **watercress.**

About 1½ quarts soup

Cream of Fresh Mushroom Soup

8 ounces fresh mushrooms, cleaned and sliced
¼ cup butter or margarine
2 tablespoons chopped onion
½ cup flour
½ teaspoon salt
⅛ teaspoon pepper
3 cups chicken broth (homemade, canned, or from bouillon cubes)
2 cups milk
2 tablespoons sherry

1. Put mushrooms into an electric cooker.
2. Heat butter in a saucepan. Mix in onion and cook until crisp-tender. Mix in flour, salt, and pepper. Add chicken broth gradually, stirring constantly. Continue to stir and bring to boiling. Pour into cooker with mushrooms.
3. Cover and cook on High 2½ to 3 hours.
4. Add milk to cooker; stir.
5. Cover and cook on Low 1 hour.
6. Just before serving, stir in sherry. Garnish with **snipped parsley.**

About 2½ pints soup

Black Mushroom-Wine Soup

2 ounces (about 1 cup) dried mushrooms (black Italian variety), broken into small pieces
¾ cup chopped onion
½ cup chopped celery
1 medium garlic clove, minced
1 bay leaf
8 peppercorns
Few sprigs parsley
¾ teaspoon Worcestershire sauce
2 quarts beef broth (homemade or made from bouillon cubes)
3 tablespoons cornstarch
½ cup cold water
¾ cup sauterne

1. Put mushrooms, onion, and celery into an electric cooker. Add garlic, bay leaf, peppercorns, parsley, Worcestershire sauce, and broth.

2. Cover and cook on Low 6 hours, or until vegetables are tender.

3. Blend cornstarch and cold water until smooth. Gradually add to mushroom soup mixture, stirring constantly.

4. Cover and cook on High 30 minutes.

5. Strain soup through sieve or colander, lightly pressing mushrooms against sieve with back of spoon to extract as much soup as possible. Discard contents of sieve.

6. Mix sauterne into strained soup and serve.

6 to 8 servings

French-Canadian Onion Soup

7½ cups well-seasoned beef broth or stock (preferably homemade)
  3 large onions, peeled and thinly sliced
  ½ cup butter
1½ tablespoons flour
    Salt and pepper to taste
    Few drops Tabasco
  6 slices French bread, toasted
  4 ounces finely shredded Cheddar cheese

1. Put broth into an electric cooker.

2. Fry onion in butter in a skillet until golden brown. Stir in flour, salt, pepper, and Tabasco. Add to broth; stir.

3. Cover and cook on Low 4 to 6 hours.

4. Ladle soup into individual ovenproof bowls. Top each with toast and cover with cheese. Set under broiler 3 to 4 minutes, or until cheese is melted and bubbly.

About 8 servings

The slow cooker is a handy hostess tool; it doubles as a keep-warm serving dish.

Easy Vegetable Soup

¼ cup butter or margarine
½ cup diced white turnip
½ cup diced carrot
½ cup chopped celery
¼ cup chopped onion
1½ cups diced raw potato
  1 quart beef broth (from bouillon cubes) or water
  1 teaspoon salt
    Few grains pepper
  1 to 2 tablespoons chili sauce

1. Heat butter in a saucepot. Mix in turnip, carrot, celery, and onion; cook until lightly browned.

2. Turn vegetables into an electric cooker. Add potato, broth, salt and pepper; mix.

3. Cover and cook on Low 4 to 6 hours.

4. Stir chili sauce into soup before serving.

About 6 servings

Squash Soup

  2 cups mashed cooked squash, or 2 packages (10 ounces each) frozen squash, thawed
  3 large onions, peeled and chopped
  2 stalks celery, chopped
  1 clove garlic, finely minced
  2 tablespoons chopped parsley
  ½ teaspoon rosemary
  ½ teaspoon savory
  1 quart chicken stock (homemade, canned, or from bouillon cubes)
  2 cups half-and-half
    Salt, pepper, nutmeg

1. Combine all ingredients, except half-and-half, in an electric cooker.

2. Cover and cook on low 4 to 6 hours, or until vegetables are tender.

3. Turn to Off and stir in half-and-half. Add salt and pepper to taste; sprinkle with nutmeg and serve.

About 6 servings

Brussels Sprout Chowder

¼ pound salt pork, diced
1 large onion, peeled and sliced
3 large potatoes (about 1½ pounds), pared and diced
2 packages (10 ounces each) frozen Brussels sprouts, defrosted and cut in halves
½ teaspoon basil or marjoram, crushed
1 teaspoon salt
⅛ teaspoon pepper
2 cups boiling water
1 quart milk
⅓ cup flour
⅓ cup cold water

1. Cook salt pork in a large skillet over medium heat about 3 minutes, stirring occasionally. Add onion and cook until pork and onion are lightly browned.
2. Turn contents of skillet into a large electric cooker. Add potato, Brussels sprouts, seasonings, and boiling water.
3. Cover and cook on Low 4 to 6 hours.
4. Turn cooker control to High. Stir in milk.
5. Combine flour and cold water in a jar; cover tightly and shake well to blend. Add flour-water mixture to hot chowder, stirring constantly; cook and stir until slightly thickened.

About 3 quarts soup

Vegetable Soup Italienne

2 tablespoons butter
2 tablespoons vegetable oil
1 cup thinly sliced carrot
1 cup thinly sliced zucchini
1 cup thinly sliced celery
1 cup finely shredded cabbage
2 beef bouillon cubes
2 quarts boiling water
2 teaspoons salt
2 medium tomatoes, cut in pieces
½ cup uncooked broken spaghetti
½ teaspoon thyme

1. Heat the butter and oil in a saucepot. Add the carrot, zucchini, celery, and cabbage. Cook, uncovered, about 10 minutes, stirring occasionally.
2. Turn contents of saucepot into an electric cooker. Add the bouillon cubes, water, and salt; mix.
3. Cover and cook on Low 4 to 6 hours.
4. Add tomatoes, spaghetti, and thyme to cooker; stir.
5. Cover and cook on Low 1 hour. Serve hot with **shredded Parmesan cheese** sprinkled over the top of each serving.

About 6 servings

Spiced Fresh Tomato Cream Soup

8 firm ripe tomatoes, cut in quarters
1 onion, peeled and quartered
2 tablespoons sugar
½ teaspoon salt
¼ teaspoon pepper
¼ teaspoon cinnamon
⅛ teaspoon cloves
1 bay leaf
2 vegetable bouillon cubes, crushed
½ cup Thick White Sauce (see recipe)
1 cup half-and-half

1. Put tomatoes and onion into an electric cooker. Add seasonings including bouillon; mix.
2. Cover and cook on Low 4 to 6 hours.
3. Strain contents of cooker through a cheese-cloth-lined sieve.

4. Stir about 1 cup hot liquid into hot white sauce. Pour into cooker and add remaining liquid and the half-and-half; mix well.

5. Cover and cook on Low 1 hour.

About 4 servings

Thick White Sauce: Heat **1½ tablespoons butter** or **margarine** in a saucepan. Blend in **1½ tablespoons flour, ⅛ teaspoon salt,** and **few grains pepper.** Heat until bubbly. Add **½ cup milk** gradually, stirring constantly. Bring to boiling; cook and stir 1 to 2 minutes.

½ cup sauce

Pea Soup à la Française

   1 **small head lettuce, shredded (about 5 cups)**
   2 **cups shelled fresh green peas, or one**
       10-ounce package frozen green peas
   1 **cup water**
   ½ **cup chopped leek (green part only)**
   2 **tablespoons butter**
   2 **teaspoons chervil**
   1 **teaspoon sugar**
   1 **teaspoon salt**
   ¼ **teaspoon black pepper**
   1 **can (about 10 ounces) condensed beef broth**
   ¾ **cup water**
   2 **cups half-and-half**

1. Put lettuce, peas, 1 cup water, leek, butter, chervil, sugar, salt, and pepper into an electric cooker; stir.

2. Cover and cook on Low 4 to 6 hours.

3. Press mixture through a coarse sieve or food mill and return to cooker. Stir in broth, ¾ cup water, and half-and-half.

4. Cover and cook on Low 1 hour.

6 servings

The more you vary your crock cooking, the more enjoyable it will be. Don't typecast the crock as a "stew cooker." Experiment with homemade soups, chowders, and the many main dishes you'll find in this book. Branch out and try the breads and desserts, too. Baking in the cooker won't heat up the kitchen as much as the standard oven.

Cream of Potato-Leek Soup

   3 **medium potatoes, pared and diced**
   2 **leeks, washed and diced (include some**
       green tops)
   1 **teaspoon salt**
   ⅛ **teaspoon white pepper**
   1 **cup chicken broth (1 chicken bouillon cube**
       dissolved in 1 cup boiling water)
   1½ **cups half-and-half**
   2 **tablespoons snipped chives**
   ¼ **teaspoon paprika**

1. Put potato, leek, salt, pepper, and broth into an electric cooker; stir.

2. Cover and cook on Low 4 to 6 hours.

3. Sieve contents of cooker or purée in an electric blender. Return to cooker and add half-and-half; mix.

4. Cover and cook on Low 1 hour.

5. Garnish soup with chives and paprika.

About 4 servings

Harvest Soup

8 slices bacon, cut in 1- to 2-inch pieces
2 cloves garlic, minced
¾ cup uncooked rice
1 teaspoon oregano, crushed
1 teaspoon salt
½ teaspoon pepper
1 package (10 ounces) frozen peas and carrots, defrosted
4 packages (10 ounces each) frozen Brussels sprouts, defrosted and quartered
5 cups chicken broth (dissolve 7 chicken bouillon cubes in 5 cups boiling water)
1½ quarts milk
¾ cup shredded Parmesan cheese

1. Fry bacon with garlic in a skillet until bacon is partially cooked.
2. Put garlic and bacon into a large electric cooker. Add rice, seasonings, peas and carrots, Brussels sprouts, and broth; stir.
3. Cover and cook on Low 4 to 6 hours.
4. Stir milk into soup.
5. Cover and cook on Low 1 hour.
6. Stir cheese into soup before serving.

About 4½ quarts soup

Mixed Fruit Soup

¼ cup pearl tapioca
2 cups water
1¼ cups (8 ounces) dried prunes
¾ cup (4 ounces) dried apricots
1 cup (about 5 ounces) seedless raisins
1 cup sugar
¼ teaspoon salt
2 pieces stick cinnamon (about 4 inches)
3 large apples, cored and cut in pieces
1 lemon, sliced and cut in half slices
1 orange, sliced and cut in half slices
1½ quarts water
¼ cup maraschino cherries

1. Put tapioca and 2 cups water into a small saucepan. Cover; set aside to soak overnight.
2. The next day, bring tapioca to boiling and cook, uncovered, stirring frequently, about 45 minutes, or until the tapioca is clear.
3. Rinse dried fruits and put into an electric cooker. Add cooked tapioca, sugar, salt, cinnamon, apple, lemon, orange, and 1½ quarts water; stir well.
4. Cover and cook on Low 2 to 3 hours.
5. Stir cherries into soup; serve hot or chilled.

About 3 quarts soup

Chili-Potato Soup

2 slices bacon
¾ cup chopped onion
3 medium potatoes, pared and diced
1 teaspoon salt
2 cups boiling water
2½ cups milk
1 teaspoon chili powder
¼ teaspoon oregano
⅛ teaspoon garlic salt
Few grains pepper

1. Fry bacon in a skillet until crisp. Drain on absorbent paper, crumble, and set aside.
2. Add onion to bacon fat and cook until soft.
3. Put onion, potato, salt, and water into an electric cooker.
4. Cover and cook 4 to 6 hours.
5. Purée contents of cooker and return to cooker. Add milk and seasonings; stir.
6. Cover and cook on Low 1 hour.
7. Top each serving with crumbled bacon and **shredded Parmesan cheese.**

6 servings

Cheese Soup

2 tablespoons finely chopped onion
2 tablespoons butter
3 tablespoons flour
2 cups chicken broth (homemade, canned, or from bouillon cubes)
½ cup finely chopped celery
½ cup grated carrot
1½ cups milk
1½ cups shredded sharp Cheddar cheese (6 ounces)
¼ cup croutons

1. Sauté onion in butter in a saucepan. Stir in flour. Add chicken broth gradually, stirring until smooth.
2. Turn sauce into an electric cooker. Add celery and carrot; stir.
3. Cover and cook on Low 4 to 6 hours.
4. Add milk and cheese to soup; stir.
5. Cover and cook on Low 1 hour.
6. Serve topped with croutons.

About 1 quart soup

MAIN DISHES

Be not angry or sour at table;
whatever may happen put on a cheerful mien,
for good humor makes one dish a feast.

From a Shaker manual, *Gentle Manners*

Beef, Burgundy Style

2 pounds beef round steak, cut in 1-inch cubes
2 tablespoons flour
1½ teaspoons salt
½ teaspoon pepper
¼ cup butter or margarine
1 cup chopped onion
½ cup chopped carrot
1 clove garlic, minced
1 cup water
3 sprigs parsley, chopped
1 bay leaf
¼ teaspoon marjoram
2 potatoes, pared and cut in pieces
2 cups burgundy or other dry red wine

1. Coat meat with a mixture of flour, salt, and pepper. Brown meat cubes in 2 tablespoons butter in a large skillet. Set browned meat aside.
2. Add remaining butter to skillet and brown onion, carrot, and garlic. Turn into an electric cooker.
3. Add water to skillet and heat, stirring to loosen browned particles.
4. Put meat, parsley, bay leaf, and marjoram into cooker. Pour liquid in skillet over all.
5. Cover and cook on Low 4 hours.
6. Add potato to cooker; stir.
7. Cover and cook on Low 2 hours.
8. Add wine to cooker; mix.
9. Cover and cook on High 30 minutes.

6 to 8 servings

Multi-Vegetable Beef Stew

3 pounds lean beef for stew (1½-inch cubes)
⅓ cup flour
1 teaspoon salt
½ teaspoon pepper
   Fat
6 small potatoes, pared
6 green onions with tops, sliced
3 large carrots, pared and cut in ½-inch pieces
3 large stalks celery, cut in ½-inch pieces
¼ pound green beans, ends trimmed and beans cut in 1-inch pieces
1 can (16 ounces) tomatoes (undrained)
1 can (about 10 ounces) condensed beef broth
½ cup dry red wine

1. Coat beef cubes with a mixture of flour, salt, and pepper; brown in fat in a large skillet.
2. Put browned meat into an electric cooker. Add vegetables, broth, and wine; mix well.
3. Cover and cook on Low 10 to 12 hours.

10 to 12 servings

Vegetable Beef Stew

2 pounds lean beef for stew (1-inch cubes)
   Vegetable oil
4 large carrots, pared and sliced
3 medium potatoes, pared and cut in ½-inch cubes
2 onions, peeled and sliced
2 stalks celery, cut diagonally in pieces
1 can (16 ounces) tomatoes (undrained)
2 teaspoons salt

1. Brown beef in oil in a large skillet.
2. Layer vegetables in an electric cooker. Sprinkle with salt. Top with browned meat.
3. Cover and cook on Low 10 to 12 hours.

About 8 servings

Homestyle Beef Stew

    4 medium carrots, pared and thinly sliced
    3 medium potatoes, pared and diced
    2 medium onions, peeled and sliced
    2 teaspoons salt
    2 to 3 pounds lean beef for stew (1-inch
        cubes)
      Flour and salt
      Cooking oil
 1½ cups canned beef broth, consommé, or part
        broth and part dry red wine
    3 tablespoons butter or margarine, softened
    3 tablespoons flour

1. Layer vegetables in an electric cooker. Sprinkle with salt.
2. Coat beef with a mixture of flour and salt; brown in oil in a large skillet. Spoon beef cubes onto vegetables. Add broth to skillet; heat; stirring to loosen browned particles. Pour broth into cooker.
3. Cover and cook on Low 8 to 10 hours.
4. To thicken gravy, make a paste of butter and flour. Add to stew liquid; stir to blend.
5. Cover and cook on High 1 hour.

8 to 12 servings

Beef Stew with Dumplings

Stew:
    2 cups beef broth (2 beef bouillon cubes
        dissolved in 2 cups boiling water)
   ¼ cup quick-cooking tapioca
    1 pound lean beef for stew (1-inch cubes)
    2 carrots, pared and cut in pieces
    2 stalks celery, sliced
    1 large onion, peeled and chopped
   ½ teaspoon salt
    1 teaspoon paprika
Dumplings:
   ¾ cup flour
    1 teaspoon baking powder
   ¼ teaspoon salt
    1 tablespoon shortening
    1 egg, beaten
   ⅓ cup milk

1. For stew, put broth and tapicoa into an electric cooker; mix. Let stand 5 minutes. Add remaining stew ingredients; mix.
2. Cover and cook on Low 10 to 12 hours.

3. Turn cooker control to High.
4. For dumplings, blend flour, baking powder, and salt. Cut in shortening until mixture is crumbly. Mix egg and milk, add to dry ingredients, and stir with a fork just until moistened. Drop by tablespoonfuls onto bubbling stew.
5. Cover loosely and cook on High 15 to 30 minutes.

About 4 servings

Stifado

    2 pounds lean beef for stew (1½-inch cubes)
      Cooking oil
    2 pounds small white onions, peeled
    1 bay leaf
    2 teaspoons salt
   ½ teaspoon cloves
   ¼ teaspoon allspice
   ¼ teaspoon pepper
    1 can (8 ounces) tomato sauce
   ½ cup dry red wine
    2 cloves garlic, crushed

1. Brown meat in oil in a large skillet.
2. Combine meat and remaining ingredients in an electric cooker.
3. Cover and cook on Low 8 to 10 hours, or until meat is tender.
4. Serve with noodles, if desired.

About 8 servings

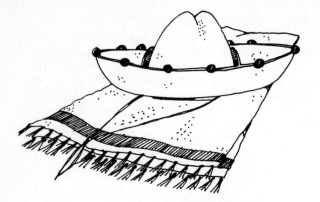

Beef and Kidney Beans Southwestern Style

1½ pounds beef round steak, cut in 1-inch
       pieces
  2 tablespoons olive oil or other cooking oil
  3 onions, peeled and coarsely chopped
  2 large cloves garlic, minced
  1 teaspoon salt
  ¼ teaspoon pepper
  1 cup canned beef broth
  1 can (8 ounces) tomato sauce
  1 can (16 ounces) tomatoes (undrained)
  2 cans (about 16 ounces each) red kidney
       beans, drained and rinsed
  1 can (5½ ounces) pitted ripe olives, drained

1. Brown meat in oil in a large skillet. Remove beef with slotted spoon and put into an electric cooker.
2. Add onion and garlic to fat in skillet and cook until lightly browned. Add to cooker and sprinkle with salt and pepper. Add broth and stir.
3. Cover and cook on Low 8 to 10 hours.
4. Stir in tomato sauce, tomatoes, and kidney beans
5. Cover and cook on Low 1 hour.
6. Before serving, stir in ripe olives.
7. Ladle into bowls.

About 8 servings

Oxtail Stew

  ½ cup flour
  1 teaspoon salt
  ¼ teaspoon pepper
  3 oxtails (about 1 pound each), disjointed
  3 tablespoons butter or margarine
  1 cup chopped onion
  4 medium potatoes, pared and diced
  6 medium carrots, pared and diced
  2 teaspoons paprika
  1 teaspoon salt
  ¼ teaspoon pepper
  1 can (28 ounces) tomatoes (undrained)
  2 pounds fresh peas, shelled
  ¼ cup cold water
  2 tablespoons flour

1. Mix ½ cup flour, 1 teaspoon salt, and ¼ teaspoon pepper in a plastic bag; coat oxtail pieces evenly by shaking 2 or 3 pieces at a time.
2. Heat butter in a saucepot or Dutch oven. Add onion and cook until soft. Remove onion with a slotted spoon and set aside.
3. Brown meat on all sides in saucepot.
4. Put browned meat into an electric cooker. Add cooked onion, potatoes, carrots, paprika, remaining salt and pepper, and tomatoes.
5. Cover and cook on Low 9 to 11 hours.
6. Add peas to cooker and stir.
7. Cover and cook on Low 1 hour.
8. Turn cooker control to High.
9. Blend cold water and 2 tablespoons flour. Stir into mixture in cooker; cook and stir until slightly thickened.

6 to 8 servings

Beef Pot Roast with Vegetables

  2 to 3 potatoes, pared and sliced
  2 to 3 carrots, pared and sliced
  1 to 2 onions, peeled and sliced
  1 beef chuck under blade pot roast (about 4
       pounds)
     Salt and pepper
  ½ cup water or beef consommé

1. Put vegetables into an electric cooker.
2. Season meat with salt and pepper. Put into cooker. Add water.
3. Cover and cook on Low 8 to 10 hours, or until meat is tender.

About 6 servings

Burgoo

1 pound beef chuck, boneless, cut in pieces
¼ pound lamb shoulder, boneless, cut in pieces
1 beef soup bone, cracked
1 pound chicken breasts, thighs, or legs
1½ cups fresh whole kernel corn
1⅓ cups fresh green lima beans
1 cup diced potato
1 cup chopped onion
½ cup diced carrot
2 teaspoons salt
½ teaspoon pepper
⅛ teaspoon cayenne pepper
2 cups water
1 cup sliced okra
½ cup chopped green pepper
1 can (19 ounces) tomatoes (undrained)
1 clove garlic, crushed in a garlic press
½ cup chopped parsley

1. Put meat, soup bone, and chicken into a large electric cooker. Add corn, limas, potato, onion, carrot, salt, peppers, and water.
2. Cover and cook on Low 10 to 12 hours.
3. Add okra, green pepper, tomatoes, and garlic; stir.
4. Cover and cook on Low 1 to 2 hours.
5. Stir in parsley before serving.

About 3 quarts Burgoo

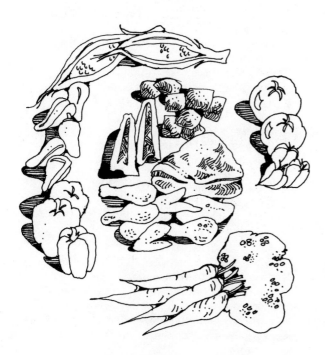

The slow cooking pot can do wonders for the food budget. That's because the slow, lengthy cooking converts less-tender (and less expensive) cuts of meat into fork-tender morsels. Watch for the special of the week at the meat counter, then choose a recipe from this book. You'll subtract from the budget—and add interest to your meals.

One-Cook Casserole

2 pounds veal round steak, cut in serving pieces
1½ tablespoons flour
½ teaspoon salt
3 tablespoons butter
4 teaspoons flour
1¼ cups canned chicken broth
½ teaspoon mustard
1½ teaspoons grated lemon peel
1 teaspoon meat extract
1 teaspoon brown sugar
½ teaspoon paprika
½ teaspoon salt
⅛ teaspoon pepper
½ clove garlic, crushed
2 tablespoons sherry
1 cup chopped onion
4 medium potatoes, pared and sliced wafer-thin

1. Rub veal with a mixture of 1½ tablespoons flour and salt.
2. Heat 2 tablespoons of the butter in a skillet; add veal and brown on both sides; put into an electric cooker.
3. Heat the remaining 1 tablespoon butter in the skillet. Stir in 4 teaspoons flour; heat until flour is browned. Add broth and cook over medium heat, stirring constantly until thickened and smooth. Stir in mustard, lemon peel, meat extract, brown sugar, paprika, salt, pepper, garlic, and sherry.
4. Sprinkle chopped onion over veal in casserole; cover with layer of thinly sliced potatoes; pour prepared gravy over potatoes.
5. Cover and cook on Low 8 to 10 hours.
6. If desired, serve with tomato halves sprinkled with chopped chives or parsley.

4 servings

Short Ribs, Western Style

- 1 cup dried lima beans, rinsed
- 1 quart water
- 3 tablespoons flour
- 1 teaspoon dry mustard
- 2 tablespoons fat
- 2 pounds beef rib short ribs, cut in serving-size pieces
- 3 medium onions, peeled and quartered
- 1 teaspoon salt
- ⅛ teaspoon pepper

1. Put beans into an electric cooker, add water, cover, and let stand overnight.
2. The next day, blend flour and dry mustard; coat short ribs evenly.
3. Heat fat in a large skillet and brown ribs on all sides.
4. Add brown ribs to soaked limas. Add onion and seasonings.
5. Cover and cook on Low 8 to 10 hours.

About 6 servings

Spiced Short Ribs with Cabbage

- 3 pounds lean beef short ribs
- ½ cup flour
- 1 tablespoon salt
- ½ teaspoon pepper
  Fat
- 1 medium onion, peeled and sliced
- ½ cup sliced celery
- 1 tablespoon dry mustard
- ½ teaspoon crushed oregano
- ⅛ teaspoon crushed sage
- 1 bay leaf
- 1 cup canned beef broth
- ½ head cabbage, cut in 4 wedges

1. Coat short ribs with a mixture of flour, salt, and pepper.
2. Brown meat in fat in a large skillet.
3. Put onion and celery into an electric cooker. Add browned meat and sprinkle with dry seasonings. Pour broth over all.
4. Cover and cook on Low 4 to 6 hours.
5. Add cabbage to cooker.
6. Cover and cook on Low 1 hour.

About 4 servings

Spaghetti Sauce

- 1½ pounds lean ground beef
- ½ cup chopped onion
- 1 clove garlic
- 1 tablespoon sugar
- 1 teaspoon salt
- 1 teaspoon oregano
- 1 teaspoon dried parsley flakes
- ¼ teaspoon anise
- 1 medium bay leaf
- 1 tablespoon grated Parmesan cheese
- 1 can (16 ounces) tomatoes (undrained)
- 1 can (6 ounces) tomato paste

1. Brown beef in a skillet; drain off any excess fat.
2. Put browned meat into an electric cooker and add remaining ingredients; stir thoroughly.
3. Cover and cook on Low 10 to 12 hours.
4. Serve sauce over **cooked spaghetti.**

About 8 servings

Italian Spaghetti Sauce

- ¼ cup olive oil
- 1 cup finely chopped onion
- 4 cloves garlic, crushed
- 1 pound ground beef
- ½ pound ground veal
- ½ pound sweet Italian sausage, cut in small pieces
- 1 can (28 ounces) Italian-style tomatoes (undrained)
- 2 cans (6 ounces each) tomato paste
- 1 can (about 10 ounces) condensed tomato soup
- ½ cup water
- ¾ cup dry red wine
- 1½ teaspoons Worcestershire sauce
- 1 teaspoon salt
- 1 teaspoon sugar
- ½ teaspoon celery salt
- ¼ teaspoon crushed red pepper
  Dash each chili powder, cinnamon, fennel seed, and oregano
- 2 small bay leaves
- 4 whole allspice, crushed
- ¾ cup chopped green pepper
- ½ pound fresh mushrooms, cleaned and sliced lengthwise
- ½ cup chopped pimento-stuffed olives
- 1 jar (4 ounces) pimentos, drained and chopped

1. Heat the olive oil in a large skillet. Add the onion and garlic and cook until onion is tender, about 5 minutes. Add the beef, veal, and sausage; brown well.
2. Remove browned mixture with slotted spoon to an electric cooker. Add remaining ingredients, except mushrooms, olives, and pimentos; stir.
3. Cover and cook on Low 10 to 12 hours.
4. Remove bay leaves. Stir in mushrooms, olives, and pimentos; heat thoroughly.
5. Serve sauce over **cooked spaghetti** and top with grated **Romano cheese**.

About 2 quarts sauce

Liquids don't boil away in crock cooking; that is why you need never fear burned food. To avoid ending up with too much liquid when converting a recipe to a slow cooker one, use only half the amount called for in the recipe.

Lemony Meat Sauce with Spaghetti

  2 **pounds ground beef**
 ¾ **cup finely chopped onion**
 ½ **cup chopped green pepper**
  2 **cloves garlic, crushed**
 ¼ **cup firmly packed brown sugar**
  1 **teaspoon salt**
 ¼ **teaspoon pepper**
  1 **teaspoon thyme**
 ½ **teaspoon basil**
  2 **cans (8 ounces each) tomato sauce**
  2 **cans (6 ounces each) tomato paste**
  1 **can (6 ounces) sliced broiled mushrooms (undrained)**
  1 **tablespoon grated lemon peel**
 ¼ **cup lemon juice**

1. Put meat, onion, green pepper, and garlic into a heated large saucepot. Cook until meat loses its pink color.
2. Remove mixture from saucepot with a slotted spoon and put into an electric cooker. Add brown sugar, seasonings, and tomato sauce and paste; mix well.
3. Cover and cook on Low 10 to 12 hours.

4. Stir in mushrooms, lemon peel, and lemon juice; heat thoroughly.
5. Spoon sauce over hot spaghetti and accompany with shredded Parmesan cheese.

10 to 12 servings

Chili con Carne

  2 **pounds ground beef (chuck)**
  1 **to 2 tablespoons chili powder**
  1 **tablespoon onion flakes**
  1 **teaspoon salt**
 ½ **teaspoon cinnamon**
 ½ **teaspoon cumin**
 ½ **teaspoon allspice**
 ¼ **teaspoon garlic salt**
 ¼ **teaspoon red pepper**
 1½ **tablespoons vinegar**
  2 **teaspoons Worcestershire sauce**
  1 **can (about 15 ounces) kidney beans (undrained)**
  1 **can (6 ounces) tomato paste**
  1 **cup water**

1. Brown beef in a skillet; drain off excess fat.
2. Put browned meat into an electric cooker. Add remaining ingredients; stir.
3. Cover and cook on Low 6 to 8 hours.

8 to 10 servings

Chili and Beans

- 2 pounds dried beans (pink, red, or pinto), rinsed
- 2 medium onions, peeled and sliced
- 1 tablespoon salt
- 9 cups water
- 1 tablespoon cooking oil
- 2 cloves garlic, crushed
- 2 pounds coarsely ground beef
- 1 can (28 ounces) whole tomatoes (undrained)
- 1 cup chopped celery
- 2 to 3 teaspoons chili powder (or more to taste)
- 1 teaspoon paprika
- 1 teaspoon dry mustard
- 1 tablespoon salt

1. Put beans into a large saucepot or Dutch oven. Add 3 quarts water. Cover and let stand overnight.
2. The next day, drain off water. Put beans, onion, and 1 tablespoon salt into a large electric cooker. Add 9 cups water.
3. Cover and cook on Low 6 to 8 hours.
4. Meanwhile, heat oil in a large skillet. Add garlic and meat; cook until meat no longer appears pink. Stir in tomatoes, celery, and dry seasonings.
5. Add meat sauce to beans; mix.
6. Cover and cook on Low 1 hour.

About 3 quarts chili

Lima Bean Chili con Carne

- 1 pound ground beef
- ½ cup chopped onion
- ⅓ cup coarsely chopped celery
- ¼ cup green pepper strips
- 1 tablespoon chili powder
- 1 teaspoon sugar
- ½ teaspoon salt
- ¼ teaspoon celery seed
- ⅛ teaspoon pepper
- ⅛ teaspoon savory
- 2½ cups drained canned tomatoes, cut in pieces
- 1 can (17 ounces) green lima beans, drained
- 1 can (17 ounces) whole kernel corn, drained

1. Brown beef in a skillet; drain off excess fat.
2. Put browned meat and remaining ingredients into an electric cooker.
3. Cover and cook on Low 6 to 8 hours.

About 8 servings

Spanish Rice

- 3 tablespoons olive oil
- 2 large onions, peeled and finely chopped
- 2 green peppers, cleaned and finely chopped
- 1 clove garlic, peeled and minced
- 2 pounds ground round steak or chuck
- 2 cans (28 ounces each) Italian-style tomatoes (undrained)
- 1 can (6 ounces) tomato paste
- 1 tablespoon wine vinegar
- 1 tablespoon Worcestershire sauce (optional)
- 1 dash Tabasco (optional)
- 2 teaspoons salt
  Pepper to taste
- 1½ teaspoons chili powder
  Few grains cayenne pepper
- 1 bay leaf
- 2 or 3 whole cloves
- 2 cups uncooked long grain rice

1. Heat olive oil in a large skillet. Add onion, green pepper, and garlic; cook over medium heat until tender and lightly browned. Remove vegetables with a slotted spoon to an electric cooker.
2. Add meat to oil remaining in skillet. Cook over medium heat until lightly browned, stirring occasionally. Add to cooker with tomatoes, tomato paste, vinegar, Worcestershire sauce, Tabasco, salt, pepper, chili powder, cayenne pepper, bay leaf, cloves, and rice; stir thoroughly to blend well.
3. Cover and cook on Low 4 to 6 hours.

8 to 10 servings

The High setting which keeps the food at a temperature around 300°F is a convenience feature. It cooks in half the time of the Low setting and helps when you need to speed things up.

Barley Beef Stew

3 pounds lean ground beef
2 teaspoons salt
¼ teaspoon pepper
2 tablespoons vegetable oil
6 onions, peeled and chopped (about 2¼ cups)
1 cup chopped celery
1 cup regular barley
2 tablespoons chili powder
1 quart tomato juice
1 cup water

1. Mix beef with salt and pepper. Heat the oil in a large heavy saucepot. Add the beef and onion, separating the meat into pieces; cook about 5 minutes, stirring occasionally. Skim off any excess fat, if desired.
2. Turn contents of saucepot into an electric cooker. Stir in celery, barley, chili powder, tomato juice, and water.
3. Cover and cook on Low 12 to 14 hours.
4. Serve in soup plates or over **toasted buns.**

3½ quarts stew

Beef-and-Rice Stuffed Peppers

6 medium green peppers
1 pound lean ground beef
⅓ cup chopped onion
⅓ cup uncooked regular rice
½ cup milk
1 egg
½ teaspoon salt
¼ teaspoon pepper
½ teaspoon chili powder
1 can (about 10 ounces) condensed tomato soup
1 soup can water

1. Cut a slice from each green pepper. Remove white fiber and seeds.
2. Brown beef in a skillet; remove excess fat if necessary. Add onion, rice, milk, egg, salt, pepper, and chili powder; mix well. Spoon meat mixture into green peppers.
3. Put pepper tops in bottom of an electric cooker and set filled peppers on top.
4. Blend soup and water. Pour over peppers.
5. Cover and cook on Low 6 hours.

6 servings

Hot Cheese 'n' Beef Dip

1½ pounds lean ground beef
2 pounds pasteurized process American cheese food
2 onions, peeled and grated
6 or 7 hot peppers, minced
2 large tomatoes, peeled and finely chopped

1. Cook beef in a skillet until meat no longer appears pink; drain off excess fat. Put meat into an electric cooker.
2. Cut cheese into small pieces; put into cooker with remaining ingredients; stir well.
3. Cover and cook on High 1 hour, or until cheese is melted and mixture is blended.
4. Serve with dippers such as **crackers, corn chips,** or **potato chips.** Or serve spooned over **buttered toast.**

About 1½ quarts dip

Browning meat before adding it to the slow cooking pot offers some advantages. For one, it adds attractive color and flavor to the meat. And for another, it reduces the cooking time somewhat, as it partially cooks the meat before it goes into the pot. However, you can skip the browning if you are in a rush. Do trim off all fat, and wipe the meat well before cooking. This will remove surface particles and moisture normally removed during browning.

Meat and Cabbage

- 6 large cabbage leaves
- 1 pound lean ground beef
- 1 teaspoon salt
- ⅛ teaspoon pepper
- 1 egg, beaten
- 1 cup cooked rice
- ½ cup thinly sliced onion
- 1 can (about 10 ounces) condensed tomato soup
- ½ cup water
- ½ cup chopped celery
- 1 teaspoon minced parsley
- 3 tablespoons lemon juice
- 1 teaspoon sugar
- ½ teaspoon salt
- ⅛ teaspoon pepper

1. Cook cabbage leaves in boiling salted water until just tender; drain.
2. Combine beef, 1 teaspoon salt, ⅛ teaspoon pepper, egg, and cooked rice; toss lightly until well mixed. Put about ¼ cup of meat mixture onto center of each cabbage leaf. Roll up each leaf, tucking ends in toward center. Use wooden picks to fasten the leaves securely. Put rolls into an electric cooker.
3. Mix remaining ingredients for sauce and pour over cabbage rolls.
4. Cover and cook on Low 8 to 10 hours.

6 servings

Favorite Lamb Stew

- 3 pounds lamb shoulder, boneless, cut in 1½-inch cubes
- 1 pound potatoes, pared and cut in large pieces
- 4 large carrots, cut in 1-inch pieces
- 1 medium onion, halved and thinly sliced
- 1 cup diagonally sliced celery
- 1 teaspoon salt
- ⅛ teaspoon pepper
  Herb bouquet*
- 1 can (8 ounces) tomato sauce
- ½ cup water
- 1 can (16 ounces) cut green beans, drained
- ½ pound fresh mushrooms, cleaned and sliced lengthwise
- 1 cup dairy sour cream
- 1 tablespoon flour

1. Put lamb into a large electric cooker. Add potatoes, carrots, onion, celery, salt, pepper, herb bouquet, tomato sauce, and water; mix.
2. Cover and cook on Low 8 to 10 hours.
3. Remove herb bouquet. Add green beans, mushrooms, and a blend of sour cream and flour to cooker; stir.
4. Cover and cook on High 30 to 60 minutes.
5. Garnish with snipped parsley, if desired.

6 to 8 servings

*Herb bouquet—Put **celery leaves, parsley sprigs, bay leaf, ⅛ teaspoon thyme leaves,** and **⅛ teaspoon rosemary leaves** onto a small square of cheesecloth; tie securely.

Lamb Couscous

    1 pound lamb for stew (1-inch pieces)
    ¼ cup butter or margarine
    1 onion, peeled and chopped
    1 clove garlic, crushed
    2 cups water
    1 teaspoon salt
    ¼ teaspoon pepper
    1 bay leaf
    1 tablespoon tomato paste
    1 teaspoon Tabasco
    1 kohlrabi, pared and cut in strips
    2 tomatoes, peeled and sliced
    3 carrots, pared and cut in pieces
    ½ cup green peas (fresh or thawed frozen)
    ½ pound couscous

1. Brown lamb in butter in a skillet. Add onion and garlic; cook 3 minutes.
2. Turn contents of skillet into an electric cooker. Pour water into skillet; heat and stir to loosen browned particles. Add to cooker with salt, pepper, bay leaf, tomato paste, Tabasco, and vegetables; stir.
3. Cover and cook on High 3 to 4 hours.
4. Cook couscous following package directions. Serve with the lamb and vegetables.

About 6 servings

Irish Stew

    1 pound lamb for stew (1½-inch pieces)
    3 tablespoons all-purpose flour
    1 teaspoon salt
      Pinch pepper
      Fat
    4 small onions, peeled
    3 medium potatoes, pared and cut in quarters
    2 small carrots, pared and cut in ½-inch
        pieces
    2 stalks celery with leaves, cut in ½-inch
        slices
    1 small white turnip, pared and cut in
        quarters
    ½ teaspoon salt
      Pinch pepper
    1 cup hot water

1. Coat meat with a mixture of flour, 1 teaspoon salt, and a pinch of pepper. Brown meat in fat in a skillet.
2. Put browned meat into an electric cooker. Add vegetables, remaining salt and pepper, and water; stir.
3. Cover and cook on Low 10 to 12 hours.

About 4 servings

Baked Kraut and Chops with Apples

There is a Pennsylvania Dutch legend that goes something like this—when you eat sauerkraut, pork, and apples at the beginning of the new year, good luck will be with you throughout the year.

    6 pork loin chops, cut about 1 inch thick
    1 teaspoon salt
    ¼ teaspoon pepper
    1 to 2 tablespoons brown sugar
    2 cups (16 ounces) undrained sauerkraut
    ½ cup seedless raisins
    12 small whole canned onions
    2 unpared apples, cored and cut in wedges

1. Brown chops on both sides in a large skillet. Season chops with half of the salt and pepper.
2. Meanwhile, toss a mixture of brown sugar and the remaining salt and pepper with the sauerkraut. Mix in raisins, onions, and apples.
3. Turn half of sauerkraut mixture into an electric cooker. Top with chops. Cover with remaining kraut mixture.
4. Cover and cook on Low 8 to 10 hours.

6 servings

Pork Chop-Vegetable Supper

  6 pork loin chops (about 1 inch thick)
    Fat
  2 cans (16 ounces each) cut green beans
  1 can (12 ounces) whole kernel corn
  1 tablespoon finely chopped onion
  1 teaspoon Worcestershire sauce
  1 teaspoon salt
  ¼ teaspoon pepper
  2 tablespoons cornstarch
  1 can (8 ounces) tomato sauce

1. Brown pork chops in a small amount of fat in a skillet.
2. Put vegetables and browned chops into an electric cooker. Add seasonings.
3. Mix cornstarch and a small amount of tomato sauce. Add cornstarch mixture and remaining tomato sauce to cooker; mix.
4. Cover and cook on Low 6 to 8 hours.

6 servings

Pork Chop Casserole

  6 pork loin chops, cut about 1 inch thick
  ½ cup flour
  ½ teaspoon salt
  ⅛ teaspoon pepper
  ½ cup firmly packed brown sugar
  ½ teaspoon salt
  4 medium sweet potatoes, pared and cut in ⅛-inch slices
  3 medium tart apples, quartered, cored, pared, and cut in ½-inch slices
  ¼ cup apple cider or apple juice

1. Coat chops with flour, ½ teaspoon salt, and pepper.
2. Brown chops on both sides in a lightly greased large skillet.
3. Mix brown sugar and remaining salt.
4. Arrange browned chops in an electric cooker. Layer with half of potatoes. Sprinkle with some of brown sugar mixture. Top with half of apples and sprinkle again with sugar. Repeat layers. Pour apple cider over all.
5. Cover and cook on Low 8 to 10 hours.

6 servings

Schnitz un Knepp (Apples and Buttons)

Schnitz means "cut" and to the Pennsylvania Dutch the word has come to mean cut dried apples, which when soaked and cooked, are used as stewed fruit, for pie fillings, or in this meat dish.

  1 quart dried apples (about an 8-ounce package)
  1 smoked pork shoulder roll (3 pounds)
  2 tablespoons brown sugar
Dumplings:
  2 cups all-purpose flour
  4 teaspoons baking powder
  1 teaspoon salt
  ¼ teaspoon pepper
  1 egg, well beaten
  3 tablespoons butter, melted
  ½ cup milk

1. Cover the dried apples with water; soak overnight.
2. Next day, cover smoked shoulder roll with water in a large electric cooker.
3. Cover and cook on Low 6 hours.

4. Add the apples and water in which they have been soaked.

5. Cover and cook on Low 2 to 4 hours.

6. Stir in brown sugar.

7. To prepare the dumplings, sift the flour, baking powder, salt, and pepper together into a bowl. Add a mixture of the beaten egg, melted butter, and milk all at one time; mix only until dry ingredients are moistened. Drop by tablespoonfuls onto simmering mixture.

8. Cover and cook on High 15 minutes.

8 to 10 servings

Check the yield of a recipe against the capacity of your cooker. The crock should be at least half full.

Versatile Tomato-Celery Stew

The possible uses of this stew in the menu are varied. With ham and rice among its ingredients, it is a satisfying family meal-in-a-dish; with ham omitted, it becomes a rice-vegetable accompaniment for succulent slices of canned ham; with both ham and rice omitted, it's a colorful vegetable dish to be served in sauce dishes with a main course.

   ½ cup chopped onion
   ¼ cup chopped green pepper
   1 small clove garlic, minced
   3 tablespoons butter or margarine
   ¾ pound celery, cut diagonally in 1-inch pieces
   2 cans (16 ounces each) tomatoes (undrained)
   1 teaspoon sugar
   ¼ teaspoon crushed thyme
   ⅛ teaspoon pepper
   1 vegetable bouillon cube
   2 tablespoons minced parsley
   ½ cup uncooked rice
   ¾ to 1 pound canned ham, cut in short strips

1. Cook onion, green pepper, and garlic in butter in a large skillet until onion is softened, about 2 minutes, stirring occasionally.

2. Turn contents of skillet into an electric cooker. Add celery, tomatoes, sugar, thyme, pepper, bouillon cube, parsley, and rice.

3. Cover and cook on Low 4 to 6 hours.

4. Add ham and heat thoroughly.

5. Sprinkle **shredded Parmesan cheese** over top before serving.

About 6 servings

Oven Ribs and Kraut

   2 pounds pork loin back ribs
   1 teaspoon seasoned salt
   ¼ teaspoon freshly ground black pepper
   1 medium onion, peeled and sliced
   1 can (16 ounces) sauerkraut, drained
   1 can (16 ounces) tomatoes (undrained)
   2 teaspoons caraway seed
   1 to 2 teaspoons sugar

1. Cut back ribs into serving-size pieces. Brown on all sides in a skillet.

2. Put browned back ribs into an electric cooker. Sprinkle with seasoned salt and pepper. Put onion, sauerkraut, and tomatoes into cooker. Sprinkle with caraway seed and sugar.

3. Cover and cook on Low 6 to 8 hours.

About 6 servings

Smoked Shoulder Roll and Beans

1 smoked pork shoulder roll (3 pounds)
1 quart green beans, washed and broken in 1-inch pieces
6 potatoes, washed, pared, and quartered
1 teaspoon salt
¼ teaspoon black pepper

1. Put smoked shoulder roll into an electric cooker. Add enough water to almost cover.
2. Cover and cook on Low 8 to 10 hours.
3. Add the beans, potatoes, and seasonings to cooker.
4. Cover and cook on High 1 to 2 hours.
5. Serve on a heated platter. Accompany with **cider vinegar** for a more piquant flavor.

6 servings

Ham 'n' Cabbage Dinner

4 medium potatoes, pared and sliced
6 carrots, pared and halved lengthwise, then crosswise
1 medium cabbage, cut in 8 wedges
1 smoked ham slice (2 to 2½ pounds), cut in 8 pieces
¼ cup firmly packed light brown sugar
2 tablespoons prepared mustard
2 teaspoons prepared horseradish

1. Put vegetables into an electric cooker. Spread ham pieces with a blend of brown sugar, mustard, and horseradish. Add meat to cooker.
2. Cover and cook on Low 6 to 8 hours.

About 8 servings

Milk, sour cream, and other dairy products don't take well to crock cooking. Because of the lengthy cooking times, they tend to break down. Where they are essential to a recipe, add them at the end of the cooking time and just heat through. Or use condensed cream soups at the beginning of the cooking time for a creamy look.

Szekely Goulash

1½ pounds pork shoulder, boneless, cut in 1½-inch cubes
2 tablespoons flour
2 teaspoons paprika
1½ teaspoons salt
2 tablespoons fat
2 tablespoons finely chopped onion
1 cup water
1 can (27 ounces) sauerkraut, drained
½ teaspoon caraway seed
1½ cups dairy sour cream

1. Coat meat evenly with a mixture of flour, paprika, and salt.
2. Heat fat in a skillet. Add onion and cook until soft, stirring occasionally.
3. Brown meat evenly on all sides in the hot fat; add water and stir to loosen browned particles. Turn into an electric cooker. Add sauerkraut and caraway seed; stir.
4. Cover and cook on Low 6 to 8 hours.
5. Gradually add some of the cooking liquid to sour cream, blending well. Stir into mixture in cooker. Heat thoroughly.
6. Serve in small bowls; accompany with **boiled new potatoes.**

6 to 8 servings

Rabbit Stew

1 rabbit, cleaned and disjointed
1 carrot, cut up
2 stalks celery, cut up
1 medium onion, quartered
3 cups beef broth (dissolve 2 beef bouillon cubes in 3 cups boiling water)
½ cup tomato sauce, or ½ cup strained stewed tomatoes
1 to 2 teaspoons Worcestershire sauce
3 tablespoons flour
¼ cup cold water

1. Cover rabbit pieces with cold salted water in a saucepan (2 to 3 tablespoons salt to 6 to 8 cups water). Let stand about 1 hour.
2. Drain off the water in saucepan and put rabbit pieces into an electric cooker. Add carrot, celery, onion, and broth to rabbit.
3. Cover and cook on Low 4 to 6 hours.
4. Strain the liquid and return to cooker with the rabbit. Add tomato sauce and Worcestershire sauce.
5. Cover and cook on Low 3 to 4 hours.
6. Remove rabbit to heated serving dish.
7. Turn cooker control to High. Combine flour with water and stir into the cooking liquid; cook and stir until thickened. Season to taste with salt and pepper. Pour over the rabbit or serve in a bowl.

3 or 4 servings

Turkey-Stuffed Peppers

4 medium green peppers
1 can (about 15 ounces) spaghetti in tomato sauce with cheese
1½ cups diced cooked turkey
¼ cup finely chopped onion
1 tablespoon chopped chutney
1 tablespoon snipped parsley
1 teaspoon curry powder
¼ cup shredded Parmesan cheese

1. Rinse and cut a thin slice from the stem end of each green pepper. Remove white membrane and seeds. Rinse cavities.
2. Mix spaghetti, turkey, onion, chutney, parsley, and curry powder. Fill peppers and sprinkle tops with cheese.

3. Place filled peppers on a rack in an electric cooker.
4. Cover and cook on Low 6 to 8 hours.

4 servings

Chicken with Rice

1 broiler-fryer chicken (2 to 3 pounds), cut in pieces
1 teaspoon salt
¼ teaspoon paprika
⅛ teaspoon pepper
½ cup chopped onion
1 clove garlic, crushed in a garlic press
1 large tomato, peeled and chopped
1 tablespoon minced parsley
⅛ teaspoon saffron
1 small bay leaf
1½ cups water
1 cup uncooked regular rice

1. Season chicken with salt, paprika, and pepper. Put chicken into an electric cooker. Add onion, garlic, tomato, parsley, saffron, bay leaf, and water.
2. Cover and cook on Low 6 to 8 hours.
3. Add rice to cooker; stir.
4. Cover and cook on High 1 hour, or until rice is tender.

6 to 8 servings

Cheesy Tuna-Onion Fondue

> 2 cans (6½ or 7 ounces each) tuna, drained and flaked
> 1 pound pasteurized process American cheese, shredded (4 cups)
> ½ cup milk
> 3 tablespoons chopped parsley
> 1 tablespoon instant minced onion

1. Combine all ingredients in an electric cooker, mixing well.
2. Cover and cook on Low 2 to 3 hours, stirring after 1 hour.
3. Serve with dippers such as **crackers, corn chips,** or **potato chips.** Or serve spooned over **buttered toast.**

About 6 servings

Tripe Creole

> 2 pounds fresh beef tripe
> 2 onions, peeled and thinly sliced
> 1 large clove garlic, minced
> ¼ cup finely chopped lean ham
> 6 tomatoes, peeled and coarsely chopped
> 1 green pepper, thinly sliced
> ¼ teaspoon thyme
> 1 small bay leaf
> Few grains cayenne pepper

1. Wash the tripe thoroughly in cold water; drain. Put into an electric cooker and add salted water to cover (1 teaspoon salt per 1 quart water).
2. Cover and cook on Low 8 to 10 hours.
3. Drain tripe and cut into 2×½-inch strips.
4. Put tripe into cooker with onion, garlic, ham, tomatoes, green pepper, thyme, bay leaf, and cayenne.
5. Cover and cook on Low 4 to 6 hours.

6 to 8 servings

> **C**heck the recipe timing to make sure it fits your time schedule for the day.

Shrimp Jambalaya

> ½ cup chopped onion
> ½ cup chopped green onion
> ½ cup chopped celery
> ¼ cup chopped parsley
> ¼ pound diced cooked ham
> 2 cloves garlic, crushed in a garlic press
> ½ teaspoon salt
> ¼ teaspoon leaf thyme
> ⅛ teaspoon pepper
> ⅛ teaspoon cayenne pepper
> 1 bay leaf
> 1 cup uncooked regular rice
> 2 tablespoons vegetable oil
> 2 cups chicken broth
> 3 cans (4½ ounces each) shrimp, drained and rinsed under running cold water
> 3 large tomatoes, peeled and coarsely chopped (about 5 cups)
> ½ cup coarsely chopped green pepper

1. Combine all ingredients, except shrimp, tomato, and green pepper in an electric cooker, mixing well.

2. Cover and cook on Low 6 to 8 hours.
3. Remove bay leaf. Add shrimp, tomato, and green pepper to cooker; mix.
4. Cover and cook on Low 1 hour.

6 to 8 servings

Note: If desired, ¼ pound hot sausage, sliced and cooked, may be substituted for ham.

Beans and Franks

**2 packages (10 ounces each) frozen lima
   beans, thawed
½ cup chopped onion
1 small clove garlic, crushed in a garlic press
1 tablespoon sugar
2 teaspoons prepared mustard
½ teaspoon Worcestershire sauce
1 can (about 10 ounces) condensed tomato
   soup
3 frankfurters, cut in ¼-inch slices**

1. Combine thawed lima beans in an electric cooker with onion, garlic, sugar, mustard, Worcestershire sauce, and condensed soup.
2. Cover and cook on Low 4 to 6 hours.
3. Add frankfurters to cooker; mix.
4. Cover and heat thoroughly.

About 6 servings

Buckaroo Beans

**1 pound dried pinto or red beans, rinsed
½ pound salt pork, slab bacon, or smoked
   ham
2 medium onions, peeled and thinly sliced
2 large cloves garlic, crushed
1 small bay leaf
1 teaspoon salt
1 can (16 ounces) tomatoes (undrained)
½ cup coarsely chopped green pepper
2 tablespoons brown sugar
2 teaspoons chili powder
½ teaspoon dry mustard
¼ teaspoon crushed oregano or cumin
3 cups water**

1. Put beans into a saucepot or Dutch oven. Add 1½ quarts water. Cover and let stand overnight.
2. The next day, drain beans and put into an electric cooker.
3. Depending on meat used, wash salt pork thoroughly; slice through pork or bacon twice each

way not quite to the rind; cut ham into ½-inch cubes. Add salt pork, bacon, or ham to cooker along with remaining ingredients; mix.
4. Cover and cook on High 1 hour. Turn cooker control to Low and cook 20 to 22 hours.

About 8 servings

Fisherman's Stew

**8 slices salt pork
4 cups sliced pared potatoes
2 medium onions, peeled and sliced
1 teaspoon salt
¼ teaspoon pepper
1½ cups boiling water
2 pounds frozen cod fillets, thawed and cut in
   pieces**

1. Layer salt pork, potatoes, and onion in an electric cooker; sprinkle with salt and pepper. Add 1 cup water.
2. Cover and cook on High 2 hours.
3. Add fish and remaining water; mix gently.
4. Cover and cook on High 30 minutes.

About 8 servings

Bologna Stew

¾ pound bologna
½ cup chopped onion
½ clove garlic, minced
3 tablespoons olive oil
¾ cup coarsely chopped pitted ripe olives
1 cup tomato juice
1 teaspoon Worcestershire sauce
½ teaspoon celery salt
1 can (about 15 ounces) kidney beans, drained and rinsed
1 can (about 16 ounces) whole kernel corn, drained
1 cup shredded Cheddar cheese (about 4 ounces)

1. Cut bologna into ½-inch cubes and set aside.
2. Cook onion and garlic until tender in hot oil in a saucepan, stirring occasionally. Turn into an electric cooker. Mix in bologna, olives, tomato juice, seasonings, and vegetables.
3. Cover and cook on Low 2 hours.
4. Stir in cheese just before serving.

About 6 servings

Barbecue Bean Pot

3 cans (about 16 ounces each) baked beans in tomato sauce
1 cup diced cooked ham
1 cup canned button mushrooms
1 cup ketchup
½ cup light molasses
½ cup applesauce
2 teaspoons instant coffee powder
1 teaspoon onion powder
½ teaspoon salt
½ teaspoon garlic powder
½ teaspoon dry mustard
½ teaspoon chili powder
2 teaspoons soy sauce
Pimento-stuffed olives, sliced

1. Combine all ingredients, except olives, in an electric cooker, mixing well.
2. Cover and cook on Low 4 to 6 hours.
3. Garnish beans with sliced olives.

About 12 servings

CROCKERY COOKING
PASSPORT TO INTERNATIONAL CULINARY ADVENTURE

The New World has been called the Melting Pot for its unique merger of nationalities, but now there is a contender for the title. The slow cooker becomes a melting pot, too, blending the best of the Old World cuisines with the know-how of the New.

This section is a sampler of foreign dishes translated into the slow-cooking method. Some may be recipes you've bypassed as too time-consuming. With a slow cooker, you'll probably find that they now fit your lifestyle, given a start early in the day.

Perhaps you'll discover a new recipe here or among the foreign recipes included in other sections of this book. Try them; such experimentation will widen your cooking horizons and whet your appetite for broader culinary exploration.

FRANCE/ ITALY

Whether cooking first achieved the rank of nobility in France or Italy is debatable; both cuisines have their loyalists. Certainly no collection of international recipes would be complete without their representation.

Ratatouille is a Mediterranean dish with a French name, most often associated with Provence, but with definite Italian influence. A meld of tomatoes, eggplant, and squash, with endless variations, this dish acquires its distinction through the slow development of flavor.

That is why it is especially well suited to preparation in the slow cooker. The unhurried cooking time produces a dish true to the spirit of its noble Mediterranean predecessor.

Ratatouille

> 1 medium eggplant
> ¼ cup olive oil
> 1 medium onion, peeled and thinly sliced
> 2 cloves garlic, minced
> 2 medium zucchini, sliced ½ inch thick
> 1 medium green pepper, thinly sliced
> 5 medium tomatoes, peeled and quartered, or
>   1 can (28 ounces) tomatoes, drained
> ¼ cup chopped parsley
> 2 teaspoons salt
> 1 teaspoon basil
> ½ teaspoon pepper

1. Peel eggplant and cut into 1-inch cubes.
2. Heat oil in a large saucepot. Add onion and garlic and cook until almost tender.
3. Add eggplant, zucchini, and green pepper; cook and stir 2 to 3 minutes.
4. With a slotted spoon, transfer vegetables to an electric cooker. Add tomatoes, parsley, and dry seasonings; stir.
5. Cover and cook on Low 8 to 10 hours.
6. Serve as a vegetable or a sauce for spaghetti.

6 to 8 servings

YUGOSLAVIA

In our thoroughly modern milieu, many recipes such as Sataras from Yugoslavia had joined the ranks of the endangered species.

Now, thanks to the arrival of the electric slow-cooking pot, they can be reclassified into the active recipe file. Present-day cooks can enjoy this treat, produced through unhurried, patient cooking, and not miss a stitch in the fabric of their busy lives.

Sataras is a stewlike combination of meats and vegetables, familiar in Bulgaria as well as Yugoslavia. We are told that it was originally prepared outdoors by shepherds.

In this version, three kinds of meat are combined with a medley of vegetables and seasonings to produce an intriguing interplay of flavor.

Start the recipe early in the day by browning the meat with the onion, garlic, and paprika in a skillet. Deglazing the skillet with the cooking liquid insures that every bit of the rich flavor will find its way into the finished dish.

The browned meat, onions, and seasonings are combined in the slow cooker much as those Slavs prepared Sataras in the open air. The difference is that they had to watch the pot.

At the end of the slow-cooking time, add the tomatoes and sour cream. When heated through, Sataras is ready to serve.

Sataras

½ pound beef for stew (1- to 1½-inch cubes)
½ pound lamb for stew (1- to 1½-inch cubes)
½ pound pork cubes (1- to 1½ inches)
2 tablespoons butter or margarine
3 onions, peeled and chopped
4 green peppers (seedy centers discarded), cut in pieces
1 clove garlic, crushed
1 tablespoon paprika
1 teaspoon salt
1 teaspoon cumin seed, crushed
1 cup water
3 medium tomatoes, peeled and cut in pieces
1 cup dairy sour cream

1. Brown meat on all sides in butter in a skillet. Add onion, green pepper, garlic, and paprika; stir. Cook 3 or 4 minutes.
2. Turn contents of skillet into an electric cooker. Sprinkle with salt and cumin. Add water to skillet; heat and stir to loosen browned particles. Pour into cooker; stir.
3. Cover and cook on Low 8 to 10 hours.
4. Add tomato and sour cream to stew; mix.
5. Cover and cook on High 30 minutes.
6. Serve hot with **fluffy hot rice** and **fresh vegetable salad.**

6 to 8 servings

GERMANY

Sauerbraten is pot roast with a decidedly German accent. Its popularity shows no sign of slackening in the Fatherland, and it wins new favor whenever it is repeated abroad.

Perhaps the best-known version outside Germany is the one from the Rhineland. Crumbled gingersnaps and golden raisins added during the last few minutes of cooking give it piquancy.

But it's the early stage of the recipe that makes the dish unique: those days of marinating in a vinegar-onion-spice sauce. Follow the same initial steps when using the slow cooker. Then follow these directions tailored to your appliance.

Sauerbraten

1 **beef round rump roast, boneless (about 3 pounds)**
2 **cups water**
1 **cup vinegar**
1 **teaspoon salt**
2 **onions, peeled and sliced**
1 **carrot, pared and sliced**
5 **peppercorns**
2 **whole cloves**
1 **bay leaf**
2 **juniper berries (optional)**
1 **tablespoon lard**
¾ **cup golden raisins**
5 **or 6 gingersnaps, crumbled**
1 **tablespoon grated apple**
1 **teaspoon salt**
¼ **teaspoon pepper**
1 **cup dairy sour cream**

1. Trim excess fat from roast and put meat into a large glass bowl.
2. Combine water, vinegar, salt, onion, carrot, peppercorns, cloves, bay leaf, and juniper berries (if used) in a saucepan. Bring to boiling, then set aside to cool.
3. Pour cooled marinade over meat, cover, and refrigerate 2 or 3 days; turn meat over several times during marinating.
4. Remove meat from marinade and pat dry with paper towels. Reserve marinade.
5. Heat lard in a saucepot or Dutch oven; add meat and brown well on all sides. Put meat, fat side up, in an electric cooker. Strain marinade into cooker.
6. Cover and cook on Low 8 to 10 hours.
7. Remove meat and keep warm. Turn cooker control to High.
8. Add raisins, gingersnap crumbs, apple, salt, and pepper to liquid in cooker; cook and stir until thickened. Blend in sour cream.
9. Cover and cook on High 30 minutes.
10. Slice meat and serve with gravy. Accompany with potato dumplings, if desired.

About 8 servings

TURKEY

Harem dancers, coffee, and pipes . . . mention "Turkey" and those images come to mind. But the world is more indebted to Turkey for its cuisine, rich in seasonings and combinations that pique the imagination along with the appetite.

Dolmas are among the many Turkish dishes that have found favor in the Western world. Literally translated, "dolma" means any stuffed food.

Vine leaves, stuffed with a savory rice and ground meat mixture, are among the best known of the dolma family. But peppers, onions, or any vegetable that can be hollowed out qualify as dolma wrappers, too.

In Turkey, dolmas may be allowed to cool to lukewarm in the cooking pot before serving. This practice is rarely followed in this country, where we are accustomed to serving hot dishes hot. Thanks to modern cooking conveniences, we can easily hold food at the temperatures we prefer.

Among those conveniences, of course, is the slow cooker. In this version of dolmas, green peppers are stuffed with a mixture of ground lamb, cooked rice, chopped onions, and seasonings.

After a period of slow cooking, the heat is turned up and the makings for a tart, tomatoey sour cream sauce go in. After another half hour of cooking, the dolmas are ready.

Dolmas

6 medium green peppers
¾ pound ground lamb
1 onion, chopped
2 tablespoons olive oil
1½ cups cooked rice
1 teaspoon salt
¼ teaspoon each pepper, oregano, and cumin seed
1 cup beef broth
2 teaspoons cornstarch
3 tablespoons tomato paste
1 teaspoon lemon juice
½ cup dairy sour cream

1. Slice top from each green pepper. Remove white fiber and seeds.
2. Brown lamb and onion in hot oil in a skillet. Mix in rice and dry seasonings. Fill green peppers with meat mixture.
3. Put pepper tops in bottom of an electric cooker. Set filled peppers on top. Pour in broth.
4. Cover and cook on Low 6 hours.
5. Remove peppers to a serving dish.
6. Mix cornstarch, tomato paste, lemon juice, and sour cream; pour into cooker and stir to blend. Return peppers to cooker.
7. Cover and cook on High 30 minutes.
8. Serve sauce with stuffed peppers.

6 servings

ARGENTINA

Wanderlust should be listed among the ingredients for carbonada. This stew has not only crossed continents; it has broken the time barrier of centuries, and passed between cultures as well.

Carbonada Criolla is the Argentinean translation of this dish. The "criolla" is related to the creole cooking of our own country. That means it has a French and Spanish heritage, with a bit of African magic thrown in for good measure. American Indians contributed to creole cooking, too, as seen in this recipe in the addition of pumpkin meat.

Down Argentine way, this dish is baked in a pumpkin shell. You can duplicate the effect by making it in the slow cooker, with cut-up pumpkin meat as an ingredient. Lacking fresh pumpkin, you can substitute zucchini squash, adding it near the end of the cooking time.

Carbonada Criolla

  2 **pounds veal for stew (1- to 1½-inch pieces)**
  ½ **cup flour**
  1 **teaspoon salt**
     Lard for frying
  2 **cloves garlic, crushed**
  2 **medium onions, peeled and chopped**
  2 **green peppers, cut in strips**
  1 **cup chopped celery**
  4 **potatoes, pared and cubed**
  ½ **pound pared pumpkin meat, cubed (optional)**
  2 **apples, pared and cut in wedges**
  ¼ **cup chopped parsley**
1½ **teaspoons salt**
  ½ **teaspoon thyme**
  ¼ **teaspoon marjoram**
  ⅛ **teaspoon cayenne pepper**
  6 **peppercorns**
  1 **bay leaf**
  1 **cup white wine, such as sauterne**
  1 **cup beef broth**
  1 **can (about 8 ounces) whole kernel corn, drained**
  3 **medium tomatoes, peeled and cut in wedges**
  2 **peaches, peeled and cut in wedges**
  ½ **pound grapes, halved and seeded**
  ½ **pound zucchini, washed and thinly sliced**

1. Coat veal with a mixture of flour and 1 teaspoon salt.
2. Heat a small amount of lard in a large skillet, add meat, and brown well on all sides.
3. Put browned meat into a large electric cooker.
4. Heat a small amount of lard in a skillet, add garlic, onion, and green pepper, and cook until partially tender. Turn contents of skillet into cooker. Add celery, potato, pumpkin (if used), apple, parsley, dry seasonings, wine, and broth; mix well.
5. Cover and cook on Low 8 to 10 hours.
6. Remove bay leaf. Add corn, tomatoes, peaches, grapes, and zucchini to mixture in cooker; stir.
7. Cover and cook on High 1 hour.
8. Accompany with **fluffy hot rice.**

About 10 servings

SOVIET UNION

Solianka may be Russian in origin, but it speaks a language that is universally understood. A steaming bowl of this savory soup communicates a spirit of warmth that needs no translating.

Solianka, like most soups, adapts beautifully to preparation in the slow cooker. Its base is a fish stock, made in the crock, and it combines both fresh-water fish and shellfish with a mélange of vegetables and seasonings.

A loaf of bread, a jug of wine, and Solianka—a perfect menu troika!

Solianka

 1 **whole fish (about 1 pound)**
 1 **package soup greens (or see Note, page 56)**
 1 **teaspoon salt**
 2 **cups boiling water**
 ¼ **cup butter or margarine**
 1 **medium onion, peeled and thinly sliced**
 1 **medium cucumber, pared and coarsely chopped (seeds discarded)**
 2 **medium tomatoes, peeled and cut in pieces**
 1 **teaspoon salt**
 ¼ **teaspoon white pepper**
 ⅓ **cup drained canned shrimp or lobster**
 ⅓ **cup drained canned mussels**
 1 **gherkin, thinly sliced**
 5 **pitted ripe olives, sliced**
 1 **teaspoon capers**
    Thin lemon slices, halved
    Fresh dill
    Dairy sour cream (optional)

1. Prepare fish fillets, cut in pieces, and refrigerate.
2. To prepare fish broth, put fish head, bones, and fins and soup greens into an electric cooker; add salt and boiling water.
3. Cover and cook on High 4 hours.
4. Heat butter in a skillet. Add onion and cook 5 minutes, stirring occasionally; do not brown.
5. Strain broth and return to cooker. Add onion, cucumber, tomato, salt, and pepper to broth; stir.
6. Cover and cook on High 30 minutes.
7. Add reserved fish, shrimp, mussels, gherkin, ripe olives, capers, lemon slices, and dill to cooker; mix.
8. Cover and cook on High 30 minutes.
9. Serve soup topped with sour cream, if desired.

About 6 servings

CHINA/ U.S.A.

As recipes go, chop suey is a hybrid. It was created by Chinese cooks—after they arrived in this country. That's why it is not to be found in any collection of authentic Chinese recipes; yet it has unmistakable Oriental character.

Chop suey is a combination of meats and vegetables that have been cut into small pieces and cooked quickly in the Oriental stir-fry manner. The use of soy sauce is an integral part of this dish, too.

Serving the cooked combination with fluffy rice or Chinese noodles further adds to its Oriental credentials.

Now, with the advent of the slow cooker, chop suey is crossbred one step further. Because the lengthy cooking changes the dish from its traditional crisp-tender character, the name has been changed, too. Oriental Meat and Vegetable Stew retains age-old appeal in this new form.

Oriental Meat and Vegetable Stew

  2 tablespoons peanut oil or other cooking oil
½ pound mushrooms, cleaned and sliced lengthwise
½ pound roasted pork, cut in strips
½ pound cooked chicken, cut in strips
  1 can (8½ ounces) sliced bamboo shoots, drained
  1 cup diagonally sliced celery
  8 green onions, sliced
  2 cloves garlic, crushed
  2 teaspoons sugar
½ teaspoon salt
⅛ teaspoon pepper
⅛ teaspoon ginger
  3 to 4 teaspoons soy sauce
  1 cup chicken broth
  3 tablespoons sherry
  1 tablespoon cornstarch

1. Heat oil in a large skillet. Add mushrooms; stir and cook until tender. Put mushrooms into an electric cooker. If desired, brown pork and chicken strips in oil in the skillet.
2. Add pork, chicken, bamboo shoots, celery, green onion, garlic, dry seasonings, soy sauce, and chicken broth to cooker; mix well.
3. Cover and cook on High 2 to 2½ hours.
4. Mix sherry and cornstarch. Stir into mixture in cooker.
5. Cover and cook on High 30 minutes.
6. Serve with **hot fluffy rice** or **Chinese noodles.**

About 6 servings

INDIA/ENGLAND

Mulligatawny, the name given to the famous soup of India, means "pepper water." And originally, it was a simple broth seasoned with a sharp curry mixture.

But when the British Empire spread to India, the English gave it their own special stamp. In keeping with their preference for heartier fare, they added mutton and vegetables.

Word spread about mulligatawny, and soon it was adopted in Europe and elsewhere around the world. Each new location added a variation of its own.

That's why mulligatawny is served today in so many forms, ranging from a thin soup to a thick, almost stew. In this slow-cooker version, chicken is featured, but curry is the ingredient that points back to the origin of the recipe.

Mulligatawny Soup

- 1 **broiler-fryer chicken (2½ to 3 pounds), cut in pieces**
- 1 **package soup greens (or see Note)**
- 1 **onion, peeled and quartered**
- 1 **teaspoon salt**
- 1 **bay leaf**
- 1 **cup water**
- 5 **thick slices lean bacon, diced**
- 4 **tomatoes, peeled and chopped**
- ⅓ **cup flour**
- 2 **teaspoons curry powder**
  Cayenne pepper
- ½ **cup half-and-half**

1. Put chicken, soup greens, onion, salt, bay leaf, and water into an electric cooker.
2. Cover and cook on Low 4 hours.
3. Remove chicken from cooker and set aside. Strain broth and reserve 1 cup. Pour remaining broth into cooker.
4. Fry bacon in a skillet until lightly browned. Add chopped tomato and cook 2 minutes. Stir in flour and curry powder. Add reserved chicken broth gradually, stirring constantly until mixture comes to boiling. Add to broth in cooker.

5. Remove chicken meat from skin and bones and cut in strips. Add to cooker; stir.
6. Cover and cook on High 2 hours.
7. Add cayenne and half-and-half to cooker; mix well.
8. Serve soup with **toasted bread cubes.**

About 8 servings

Note: For soup greens, use all or a choice of the following vegetables: carrot, celery, leek, onion, parsnip, turnip; and herbs: parsley, tarragon, thyme.

MEAT, POULTRY, AND FISH

The corned beef is exquisitely done,
and as tender as a young lady's heart.

NATHANIEL HAWTHORNE

Beef Pot Roast

   1 **beef round rump roast or chuck blade roast (about 4 pounds)**
      Fat
   ½ **teaspoon seasoned salt**
   ¼ **teaspoon pepper**
   1 **onion, peeled and thinly sliced**

1. Brown roast in fat in a skillet or Dutch oven.
2. Put meat into an electric cooker and sprinkle with seasoned salt and pepper. Add onion.
3. Cover and cook on High 3 hours, or until meat is tender.
4. Use meat juices for gravy, if desired.

About 8 servings

Savory Pot Roast

   1 **beef chuck arm or blade pot roast (3 to 4 pounds)**
   2 **tablespoons flour**
   1 **tablespoon paprika**
   1 **teaspoon salt**
   ⅛ **teaspoon pepper**
   3 **tablespoons fat**
   4 **onions, peeled and thinly sliced**

1. Coat meat with a mixture of the flour, paprika, salt, and pepper. Brown meat on all sides in fat in a large skillet or Dutch oven.
2. Put about one third of the onion in a layer in an electric cooker. Put meat on onions and cover with remaining onion.
3. Cover and cook on Low 8 to 10 hours.

6 to 8 servings

Teriyaki Pot Roast

   1 **beef chuck arm or blade pot roast (3 to 4 pounds)**
      Vegetable oil
   ½ **teaspoon ginger**
   1 **clove garlic, minced**
   3 **tablespoons soy sauce**
   2 **onions, peeled and sliced**
   ¼ **cup hot water**

1. Brown pot roast in oil in a heavy skillet. Put browned roast into an electric cooker. Add ginger, garlic, soy sauce, onion, and water.
2. Cover and cook on Low 8 to 10 hours.
3. If desired, thicken the liquid with a small amount of cornstarch mixed to a paste with cold water. Serve meat and gravy with **hot fluffy rice** or **baked potatoes.**

6 to 8 servings

Beef in Savory Sauce

   1 **pound beef top round or sirloin steak, cut in 1-inch cubes**
   3 **tablespoons flour**
   ½ **teaspoon salt**
      Few grains black pepper
   1 **tablespoon butter or margarine**
   1 **can (about 10 ounces) beef gravy**
   2 **tablespoons orange juice**
   2 **tablespoons currant jelly**
   1 **can (4 ounces) sliced mushrooms, drained**
   2 **tablespoons sliced pimento-stuffed olives**

1. Coat meat evenly with a mixture of flour, salt, and pepper.
2. Brown meat evenly on all sides in butter in a large, heavy skillet. Turn browned meat into an electric cooker. Add gravy and remaining ingredients; stir.
3. Cover and cook on Low 6 to 8 hours, or until meat is tender.
4. Serve with **fluffy cooked rice.**

About 4 servings

Beef Bourguignon

    5 onions, peeled and sliced
      Vegetable oil
    2 pounds lean beef for stew (1-inch cubes)
    3 tablespoons flour
    1 cup dry red wine, such as burgundy
    1 beef bouillon cube
    ½ cup boiling water
    2 teaspoons salt
    ½ teaspoon marjoram
    ½ teaspoon thyme
    ¼ teaspoon pepper
    ½ pound fresh mushrooms, cleaned and sliced
      lengthwise, or 1 can (4 ounces) mushroom
      stems and pieces

1. Cook onion slices in oil in a large skillet until tender; put into an electric cooker.
2. Coat beef cubes with flour and brown slowly in skillet, about 15 minutes, adding more oil if necessary. Add meat to onions in cooker.
3. Combine wine, bouillon cube mashed in boiling water, and seasonings in skillet. Set over low heat and stir to loosen brown residue. Pour mixture over meat and onions; stir well.
4. Cover and cook on Low 6 to 8 hours, or until meat is tender.
5. Add mushrooms to beef mixture; stir.
6. Cover and cook on High 15 minutes.

8 servings

Hungarian Goulash (Gulyáshus)

    1 pound onions, peeled and sliced
    2 pounds lean beef round rump roast, cut in
      1½-inch pieces
    1 large clove garlic, crushed
    ¼ cup tomato paste
    1 tablespoon paprika
    ¼ teaspoon caraway seed
    1 teaspoon salt
    2 cups beef broth (homemade or canned)
    ¼ cup dairy sour cream

1. Put onion and beef into an electric cooker. Add garlic, tomato paste, paprika, caraway, salt, and broth; mix.
2. Cover and cook on Low 18 to 20 hours.
3. Blend sour cream into meat mixture.
4. Serve with **potatoes, bread, dumplings,** or **noodles.**

6 to 8 servings

Cola Steak

    1½ pounds beef round steak, boneless (about 1
       inch thick)
    1 tablespoon flour
    1 cup chopped onion
    ½ teaspoon salt
    ⅛ teaspoon garlic salt
    ⅛ teaspoon pepper
    ¼ cup ketchup
    ½ cup carbonated cola beverage

1. Trim fat from meat; cut into 4 portions. Coat meat with flour.
2. Put coated meat into an electric cooker. Add onion, dry seasonings, ketchup, and cola beverage.
3. Cover and cook on Low 8 to 10 hours.

4 servings

Cooker Corned Beef

    1 piece corned beef (about 3½ pounds)
    1 small bay leaf
    1 medium onion, peeled
    1 quart water

1. Put all ingredients into an electric cooker.
2. Cover and cook on High 2 hours. Skim foam.
3. Turn cooker control to Low and cook, covered, 5 to 6 hours.
4. Allow meat to cool 30 minutes in cooking liquid.

About 4 servings

Low gives the pleasant mingling of flavors and the marvelous aromas for which crock cooking is famous.

Spicy Beef Strips

1½ pounds beef round steak, cut ¼ inch thick
2 tablespoons butter or margarine
1 small clove garlic, crushed in a garlic press
2 teaspoons instant minced onion
½ teaspoon salt
   Few grains cayenne pepper
⅛ teaspoon chili powder
⅛ teaspoon cinnamon
⅛ teaspoon ground celery seed
1 tablespoon prepared mustard
½ cup strong beef broth (1 beef bouillon cube dissolved in ½ cup boiling water)

1. Cut steak into 2×½-inch strips. Brown in butter in a large skillet.
2. Turn browned meat into an electric cooker and add remaining ingredients; stir.
3. Cover and cook on Low 6 to 8 hours.
4. Serve on **hot fluffy rice.**

About 6 servings

Fruity Short Ribs

4½ pounds lean beef chuck short ribs
   Fat
⅓ cup flour
1 cup dried apricots
1 cup dried pitted prunes
¼ cup sugar
1 teaspoon salt
½ teaspoon cinnamon
¼ teaspoon allspice
⅛ teaspoon pepper
2 tablespoons cider vinegar
1½ teaspoons Worcestershire sauce
1 cup boiling water

1. Coat short ribs with flour. Brown on all sides in fat in a large skillet.
2. Put browned meat into a large electric cooker. Add dried fruit and remaining ingredients.
3. Cover and cook on Low 8 to 10 hours.
4. If desired, thicken liquid with a mixture of flour and water. Serve gravy with meat and fruit.

6 to 8 servings

Lemon Lamb Shanks

4 to 6 lamb shanks
½ clove garlic
3 tablespoons flour
1 teaspoon salt
¼ teaspoon pepper
1 teaspoon paprika
2 tablespoons shortening
2 peppercorns
1 small bay leaf, crushed
1 tablespoon grated lemon peel
½ cup lemon juice
½ cup water

1. Make a gash in each lamb shank. Cut garlic into 6 pieces and insert a garlic piece in each gash. Coat shanks with a mixture of flour, salt, pepper, and paprika.
2. Brown shanks slowly in shortening in a Dutch oven. Put browned shanks into a large electric cooker. Add peppercorns, bay leaf, lemon peel, lemon juice, and water.
3. Cover and cook on Low 8 to 10 hours.

4 to 6 servings

Chicken Lickin'-Good Pork Chops

6 pork loin chops (about 1½ pounds), cut 1 inch thick
½ cup flour
1 tablespoon salt
1½ teaspoons dry mustard
½ teaspoon garlic powder
   Vegetable oil
1 can (about 10 ounces) condensed chicken with rice soup

1. Trim fat from pork chops. Coat chops with a mixture of flour, salt, dry mustard, and garlic powder.
2. Brown chops on both sides in oil in a large skillet.
3. Put browned chops into an electric cooker.
4. Pour fat from skillet. Turn condensed soup into skillet, set over low heat, and stir to loosen brown residue. Pour soup over chops in cooker.
5. Cover and cook on Low 6 to 8 hours.

6 servings

Fresh Pear and Pork Chop Skillet

       6 pork loin chops, cut 1 inch thick
       ½ teaspoon salt
       ⅛ teaspoon pepper
       6 thin lemon slices
      12 thin onion slices
       3 Anjou pears, halved and cored
       ½ cup firmly packed brown sugar
       ¼ cup lemon juice
       ¼ cup water
       2 tablespoons soy sauce
       ¼ teaspoon ginger

1. Brown pork chops on both sides in a skillet. Drain off excess fat.
2. Put browned chops into an electric cooker. Sprinkle with salt and pepper. Add lemon and onion slices. Put pear halves on top.
3. Combine brown sugar, lemon juice, water, soy sauce, and ginger; pour over all.
4. Cover and cook on Low 6 to 8 hours.

6 servings

Spicy Pork with Herbs

       1 tablespoon fat
       3 pounds lean pork, boneless, cut in 1- to 1½-inch cubes
       2 medium onions, peeled and cut in wedges (8 from each)
       2 green peppers, cut in 1-inch pieces
       1 clove garlic, minced
       1 teaspoon seasoned salt
       ¼ teaspoon oregano
       ⅛ teaspoon pepper
       2 teaspoons cider vinegar
       1 can (16 ounces) tomatoes (undrained)
       ¼ cup water
       2 tablespoons flour

1. Heat fat in a large, heavy skillet. Add pork and brown lightly on all sides.
2. Transfer browned meat from skillet with a slotted spoon to a large electric cooker. Add onion, green pepper, garlic, seasoned salt, oregano, pepper, vinegar, and tomatoes to cooker; mix well.
3. Cover and cook on Low 6 to 8 hours.
4. Turn cooker control to High.

5. Blend water and flour until smooth; stir into mixture in cooker. Cook and stir until thickened.

10 to 12 servings

Sweet and Pungent Pork

       2 pounds lean pork, boneless, cut in 1- to 1½-inch cubes
       ¼ cup butter or margarine
       1 medium onion, peeled, quartered, and sliced
       ½ cup green pepper pieces
       ⅓ cup firmly packed brown sugar
       1 teaspoon salt
       ¼ teaspoon pepper
       ½ teaspoon coriander
       ¼ teaspoon cinnamon
       ½ cup lemon juice
       1 tablespoon soy sauce

1. Brown pork on all sides in butter in a skillet.
2. Add browned pork to an electric cooker. Add onion, green pepper, brown sugar, salt, spices, and lemon juice.
3. Cover and cook on Low 6 to 8 hours.
4. Stir in soy sauce before serving.

About 6 servings

Buffet Ham with Apricot Glaze

  8 ounces dried apricots, cut in pieces
1⅓ cups apple cider
  6 tablespoons light brown sugar
  ¼ teaspoon cinnamon
  ¼ teaspoon allspice
  ⅛ teaspoon cloves
  1 canned ham (about 3 pounds), sliced and
    tied

1. Put apricots into a bowl. Add apple cider; cover, and refrigerate overnight.
2. Purée apricot mixture in an electric blender or force through a food mill. Stir in brown sugar and spices.
3. Remove excess gelled substance from ham. Set ham on a rack in an electric cooker. Spread apricot mixture over ham.
4. Cover and cook on Low 4 to 6 hours.

About 8 servings

Barbecued Country Ribs

  3 pounds pork loin country-style ribs
  1 tablespoon instant minced onion
  1 tablespoon light brown sugar
1½ teaspoons paprika
  ½ teaspoon chili powder
  ½ teaspoon dry mustard
  ½ teaspoon salt
  ⅛ teaspoon cayenne pepper
  ½ cup tomato juice
  ¼ cup ketchup
  ¼ cup water
  2 tablespoons cider vinegar
1½ tablespoons Worcestershire sauce

1. Brown ribs on both sides in Dutch oven, heavy skillet, or saucepot, pouring off fat as it accumulates.
2. Meanwhile, prepare sauce. Blend onion, brown sugar, and dry seasonings in a saucepan. Add tomato juice, ketchup, water, vinegar, and Worcestershire sauce; mix. Bring to boiling, cover, and simmer about 10 minutes.
3. Put browned ribs into a large electric cooker. Pour hot sauce over ribs.
4. Cover and cook on Low 8 to 10 hours.

4 to 6 servings

Saucy Ribs

  3 pounds lean pork spareribs or pork loin
    back ribs, cut across ribs and in 3-inch
    lengths
  2 tablespoons dark brown sugar
1½ teaspoons seasoned salt
  ⅛ teaspoon seasoned pepper
  ½ teaspoon dry mustard
  1 cup ketchup
  ½ cup water
  3 tablespoons lemon juice
  3 tablespoons Worcestershire sauce
  2 tablespoons cider vinegar
  ¼ cup instant minced onion
  1 teaspoon prepared horseradish
  3 drops Tabasco

1. Brown ribs on both sides in Dutch oven, heavy skillet, or saucepot, pouring off fat as it accumulates.
2. Meanwhile, prepare sauce. Blend brown sugar and dry seasonings in a saucepan. Add ketchup, water, lemon juice, Worcestershire sauce, vinegar, onion, horseradish, and Tabasco; mix. Bring to boiling, cover, and simmer about 10 minutes.
3. Put browned ribs into a large electric cooker. Pour hot sauce over ribs.
4. Cover and cook on Low 8 to 10 hours.

About 4 servings

Walnut Meat Loaf

1½ pounds lean ground beef
½ cup chopped walnuts
¼ cup chopped onion
1 tablespoon chopped parsley
1 egg, fork beaten
1 teaspoon salt
¼ teaspoon paprika
¼ teaspoon marjoram leaves, crushed
⅛ teaspoon pepper
½ cup dry red wine
¼ cup milk
1 tablespoon butter
1½ tablespoons flour

1. Lightly mix all ingredients except butter and flour. Shape into a round loaf. Put into a greased electric cooker.
2. Cover and cook on Low 4 hours.
3. Remove loaf from cooker.
4. Turn cooker control to High. Mix butter and flour; add to liquid in cooker and mix well. Cook and stir until thickened.
5. Serve gravy over meat loaf.

About 8 servings

Surprise Meat Loaf

3 slices bread, torn in small pieces
½ cup milk
1 egg, fork beaten
1½ pounds lean ground beef
¼ cup finely chopped onion
2 tablespoons ketchup
1 tablespoon prepared horseradish
1 tablespoon Worcestershire sauce
1 teaspoon salt
¼ teaspoon pepper
¼ teaspoon garlic salt
2 large dill pickles
   Ketchup

1. Combine bread, milk, and egg in a bowl. Add meat, onion, ketchup, horseradish, Worcestershire sauce, and dry seasonings; mix lightly.
2. Put a third of meat mixture into a greased electric cooker; pat into an oval shape about 1 inch thick. Top with pickles placed end to end. Cover with remaining meat mixture; shape into a loaf. Spread top with desired amount of ketchup.
3. Cover and cook on Low 4 hours.

About 6 servings

Saucy Meatballs

1 cup ketchup
1 teaspoon prepared mustard
½ teaspoon Worcestershire sauce
1 tablespoon vinegar
⅔ cup red or white wine
2 eggs, beaten
½ cup milk
1 cup soft bread crumbs
1 pound lean ground beef
1 teaspoon salt
¼ teaspoon seasoned pepper
3 tablespoons minced parsley
2 tablespoons grated onion
½ teaspoon Worcestershire sauce
2 tablespoons butter or margarine

1. Put ketchup, mustard, ½ teaspoon Worcestershire sauce, vinegar, and wine into an electric cooker; mix.
2. Cover and cook on Low while preparing meatballs.
3. Mix eggs, milk, and bread crumbs in a bowl. Add meat, salt, seasoned pepper, parsley, onion, and remaining Worcestershire sauce; mix lightly. Shape into small balls.
4. Heat butter in a skillet; add meatballs and brown on all sides.
5. Add browned meatballs to sauce in cooker; mix.
6. Cover and cook on Low 4 to 6 hours.

About 6 servings

Picadillo

    2 tablespoons olive or vegetable oil
 1½ pounds ground beef
    ½ cup chopped onion
    ½ cup chopped green pepper
    2 small cloves garlic, crushed in a garlic press
    ½ cup sliced pimento-stuffed olives
    ½ cup dark seedless raisins
    2 tablespoons capers
    1 teaspoon salt
    ½ teaspoon cumin
    ⅛ teaspoon pepper
      Pinch allspice
    1 can (16 ounces) tomatoes (undrained)

1. Heat oil in a large skillet; add beef and cook until meat loses its pink color.
2. Transfer meat with a slotted spoon to an electric cooker. Add remaining ingredients; mix well.
3. Cover and cook on Low 6 to 8 hours.
4. Serve over **hot fluffy rice** and garnish with **chopped hard-cooked egg.**

About 6 servings

Meatballs in Apple-Tomato Sauce

    1 pound ground beef
    ¼ pound ground pork
    4 teaspoons grated onion
    1 egg, slightly beaten
    2 cans (8 ounces each) tomato sauce
    1 cup applesauce
    ½ cup soft bread crumbs
    ½ teaspoon salt
    ⅛ teaspoon pepper
    ⅛ teaspoon allspice
    ⅛ teaspoon nutmeg
      Flour
    2 tablespoons brown sugar
    ½ teaspoon salt
      Pinch pepper
    3 tablespoons vegetable oil
    1 clove garlic, crushed in a garlic press

1. Mix meat, onion, egg, ¼ cup each tomato sauce and applesauce, bread crumbs, ½ teaspoon salt, ⅛ teaspoon pepper, allspice, and nutmeg. Shape into balls about 1 inch in diameter. Coat with flour.
2. Combine brown sugar and remaining tomato sauce, applesauce, salt, and pepper in an electric cooker.
3. Cover and cook on Low while browning meatballs.
4. Heat oil with garlic in a large skillet; add meatballs and brown on all sides.
5. Put browned meatballs into sauce in cooker; mix.
6. Cover and cook on Low 4 to 6 hours.

About 6 servings

Swedish Meatballs

    1 can (about 10 ounces) condensed beef or
      chicken broth
    4 or 5 whole allspice
    4 or 5 slices slightly dry bread
    ¾ cup milk
    2 pounds lean ground beef, ground twice
    ¼ pound lean ground pork, ground twice
    1 medium onion, peeled and chopped
    2 eggs
    1 teaspoon salt
    ⅛ teaspoon pepper
      Flour
      Butter or margarine

1. Put broth and allspice into an electric cooker.
2. Cover and cook on Low while preparing meatballs.
3. Soak bread in milk in a large bowl. Add meat, onion, eggs, salt, and pepper; beat with electric mixer until light. Shape into balls about 1¼ inches in diameter; coat with flour.
4. Heat a small amount of butter in a large skillet; add meatballs and brown on all sides.
5. Put browned meatballs into broth in cooker.
6. Cover and cook on Low 4 to 6 hours.

About 10 servings

Ground Meat in Barbecue Sauce

     4 pounds ground beef
     2 cups chopped onion
     ¼ cup sugar
     4 teaspoons salt
     1 teaspoon pepper
     2 cups ketchup
     1 cup water
     ¼ cup prepared mustard
     ¼ cup vinegar
     ¼ cup Worcestershire sauce

1. Brown beef in a skillet and drain off excess fat.
2. Put beef and remaining ingredients into an electric cooker; stir thoroughly.
3. Cover and cook on High 4 hours.
4. Spoon into **heated buns.**

10 to 12 servings

Skillet Veal Loaf

     1 pound ground veal
     ¼ pound ham
     ½ teaspoon salt
     ⅛ teaspoon pepper
     ⅛ teaspoon cinnamon
     1 teaspoon grated lemon peel
     3 eggs, beaten
     2 tablespoons flour
     2 tablespoons olive or vegetable oil
     1 medium onion, peeled and chopped
     1 medium carrot, pared and finely chopped
     1 stalk celery, finely chopped
     2 tablespoons finely chopped parsley
     ¼ cup water

1. Have meat retailer grind veal and ham together three times.
2. Add salt, pepper, cinnamon, and lemon peel to beaten eggs; blend well. Lightly mix in meat. Turn onto waxed paper or aluminum foil and gently shape mixture into a large patty about the size of an electric cooker. Coat with flour.
3. Heat oil in a skillet. Add meat and brown on both sides.
4. When meat is browned, put into electric cooker. Add onion, carrot, celery, parsley, and water.
5. Cover and cook on Low 4 hours.
6. Place meat on a hot platter; set aside and keep hot.
7. Force the mixture in cooker through a coarse sieve, or purée in an electric blender. Serve sauce hot over meat loaf.

About 6 servings

Country Captain

     1 broiler-fryer chicken (3 to 3½ pounds), cut
        in serving-size pieces
     ¼ cup flour
     ½ teaspoon salt
        Pinch white pepper
     2 onions, peeled and finely chopped
     2 medium green peppers, seeded and chopped
     1 clove garlic, crushed in a garlic press
     ½ teaspoon salt
     ¼ teaspoon white pepper
     ¾ teaspoon curry powder
     ¼ teaspoon thyme
     5 cups undrained canned tomatoes
     2 cups hot cooked rice
     ¼ cup dried currants
     1 tablespoon chopped parsley
     ¾ cup roasted blanched almonds

1. Remove skin from chicken. Mix flour, ½ teaspoon salt, and pinch white pepper. Coat chicken pieces.
2. Put onion and green pepper into an electric cooker. Put coated chicken pieces on vegetables. Add garlic, ½ teaspoon salt, dry seasonings, and tomatoes.
3. Cover and cook on Low 8 to 10 hours.
4. Arrange chicken in center of a large heated platter and pile the hot rice around it. Stir currants and parsley into sauce remaining in cooker; pour over rice. Scatter almonds over top. Garnish with parsley sprigs, if desired.

About 6 servings

Texas-Style Barbecued Chicken

    3 to 3½ pounds chicken legs
    ⅓ cup flour
    1 teaspoon salt
    ⅛ teaspoon pepper
    2 tablespoons vegetable shortening
    ½ teaspoon paprika
    ¼ teaspoon celery seed
    1½ cups hickory-smoke-flavored barbecue
       sauce

1. Coat chicken with a mixture of flour, salt, and pepper. Brown chicken on all sides in shortening in a large skillet.
2. Put browned chicken legs into an electric cooker. Sprinkle with paprika and celery seed. Add barbecue sauce.
3. Cover and cook on Low 8 to 10 hours.

About 6 servings

Coq au Vin

    2 tablespoons butter
    2 tablespoons vegetable oil
    ¾ cup chopped green onion
    ¼ pound salt pork, finely diced
    8 pieces chicken
    ½ cup flour
    1 teaspoon salt
    ¼ teaspoon pepper
    ¼ cup brandy
    1 clove garlic, pressed
       Bouquet garni*
    6 ounces mushrooms, cleaned and sliced
    1 cup red wine, such as burgundy

1. Heat butter and oil in a skillet. Sauté onion, then add salt pork and brown it. Remove pork and onion with a slotted spoon and reserve.
2. Coat chicken with a mixture of flour, salt, and pepper.
3. Brown chicken pieces in fat remaining in skillet. Drain off any excess fat.
4. Warm brandy; pour over browned chicken and set aflame. When the flames have burned out, put the chicken into an electric cooker. Add onion, pork, garlic, bouquet garni, mushrooms, and wine.
5. Cover and cook 6 to 8 hours.
6. Remove bouquet garni and garlic.

4 servings

* Tie **1 bay leaf, 1 stalk celery** with leaves, **1 sprig parsley,** and a **pinch each thyme** and **rosemary leaves** in a small piece of cheesecloth.

Chicken Fricassee with Vegetables

    2 cups sliced carrot
    2 onions, peeled and quartered
    1 broiler-fryer chicken (about 3 pounds), cut
       in serving-size pieces
    1 teaspoon salt
    1 small bay leaf
    1 cup water
    2 crookneck squashes, cut in halves
       lengthwise
    2 pattypan squashes, cut in halves
       Green beans (about 6 ounces), tips cut off
    1 can (3½ ounces) pitted ripe olives, drained
    1 tablespoon cornstarch
    2 tablespoons water

1. Put carrot and onion, then chicken pieces, into an electric cooker. Add salt, bay leaf, and water.
2. Cover and cook on Low 4 to 6 hours.
3. Add squashes and green beans to cooking liquid.
4. Cover and cook on High 1 to 2 hours, or until chicken and vegetables are tender.
5. Remove chicken and vegetables to a warm serving dish and add olives; keep hot.
6. Blend cornstarch and 2 tablespoons water; stir into cooking liquid. Cook and stir until thickened. Pour gravy over chicken.

About 4 servings

Spicy Cooker Chicken

     3 **tablespoons butter**
     4 **pounds broiler-fryer chicken pieces (use
        breasts and legs)**
     2 **tablespoons flour**
     ½ **cup condensed chicken consommé**
     1 **can (16 ounces) fruit cocktail, drained
        (reserve ¼ cup syrup)**
     ¼ **teaspoon salt**
     ¼ **teaspoon turmeric**
     ⅛ **teaspoon each dry mustard, mace,
        cardamom, and ginger**
     4 **shreds saffron**

1. Heat butter in a large, heavy skillet. Add chicken pieces and brown on all sides. Remove chicken from skillet to an electric cooker.
2. Blend flour into drippings in skillet. Heat until bubbly. Add chicken consommé and fruit cocktail syrup gradually, stirring constantly. Continue stirring and bring to boiling. Add fruit cocktail and seasonings. Pour over chicken in cooker.
3. Cover and cook on Low 6 to 8 hours.
4. Serve with **hot fluffy rice**.

About 8 servings

Chicken in Tomato Sauce (Pollo Madrileño)

       Stewing chicken, 4 pounds, cut up
       Seasoned instant meat tenderizer
     ¼ **cup flour**
     ¼ **cup olive oil**
     2 **cloves garlic, minced**
     ½ **cup chopped onion**
     ½ **pound cooked ham, cut in julienne strips**
     1 **can (16 ounces) tomatoes (undrained)**
     1 **can (8 ounces) tomato sauce**
     2 **chicken bouillon cubes, crushed**
     ½ **teaspoon crushed basil**
     ½ **teaspoon seasoned instant meat tenderizer**
     3 **drops Tabasco**
     1 **teaspoon grated lemon peel**
     ½ **cups walnuts, chopped**
     ½ **cup pimento-stuffed olives**
       Lemon-flavored rice*

1. Rinse chicken and pat dry with absorbent

paper. Using about ½ teaspoon per pound, sprinkle tenderizer evenly over all sides of chicken pieces. To insure penetration of the tenderizer, pierce chicken deeply with a fork at ½-inch intervals. Coat with flour.
2. Heat olive oil with garlic in a large, heavy skillet; add chicken and brown pieces on all sides.
3. Put browned chicken into an electric cooker. Add onion, ham, tomatoes, and a mixture of the tomato sauce, crushed bouillon cubes, basil, tenderizer, Tabasco, and lemon peel; stir.
4. Cover and cook on Low 8 to 10 hours.
5. Add walnuts and olives to cooker.
6. Serve chicken in sauce over lemon-flavored rice in a heated serving dish. Garnish with additional stuffed olives, if desired.

About 6 servings

*Cook rice for 6 servings, following package directions. Add desired amount of **butter** or **margarine**. Toss the hot cooked rice with **1 teaspoon grated lemon peel**.

Chicken, Hunter Style

        2   **pounds chicken pieces**
        2   **tablespoons butter**
        1   **can (4 ounces) sliced mushrooms, drained**
        1   **can (16 ounces) tomatoes, drained and
                chopped**
        ¼   **cup sliced green onion**
        2   **tablespoons chopped parsley**
        ½   **teaspoon salt**
        ⅛   **teaspoon chervil**
        ⅛   **teaspoon tarragon**
            Few grains pepper
        1   **can (about 10 ounces) condensed tomato
                soup**
        ¼   **cup white wine**

1. Brown chicken in butter in a large skillet.
2. Put browned chicken into an electric cooker.
Add mushrooms, tomatoes, green onion, parsley,
salt, herbs, pepper, tomato soup, and wine.
3. Cover and cook on Low 6 to 8 hours.

4 to 6 servings

Chicken and Dumplings

        2   **broiler-fryer chickens, cut in serving-size
                pieces**
        ½   **cup chopped onion**
        ¼   **cup chopped celery**
        2   **tablespoons chopped celery leaves**
        1   **clove garlic, minced**
        ¼   **cup flour**
        2   **cups chicken broth**
        1   **teaspoon sugar**
        1   **teaspoon salt**
        ⅛   **teaspoon pepper**
        ½   **teaspoon basil leaves**
        1   **bay leaf**
        ¼   **cup chopped parsley**
            Basil Dumplings (see below)
        2   **packages (10 ounces each) frozen green
                peas, thawed**

1. Put chicken pieces into an electric cooker. Add
onion, celery, celery leaves, and garlic. Sprinkle
with flour and mix well. Add sugar, salt, pepper,
basil, bay leaf, and parsley.
2. Cover and cook on Low 8 to 10 hours.
3. Stir peas into mixture in cooker.
4. Cover and cook on High 45 minutes.

5. Shortly before cooking time is completed, prepare Basil Dumplings. Drop dumpling dough onto
stew.
6. Cover and cook on High 15 minutes, or until
dumplings are done.

About 8 servings

Basil Dumplings: Combine **2 cups all-
purpose biscuit mix** and **1 teaspoon basil leaves** in a
bowl. Add **⅔ cup milk** and stir with a fork until a
dough is formed. Proceed as directed in recipe.

Chicken Kumquat

        1   **broiler-fryer chicken (2½ to 3 pounds), cut
                in pieces**
        ½   **cup flour**
        1   **teaspoon salt**
        ¼   **teaspoon pepper**
        ½   **teaspoon rosemary leaves, crushed**
        ⅓   **cup butter or margarine**
        1   **jar (8 ounces) kumquats and syrup**
        3   **tablespoons coarsely chopped crystallized
                ginger**
        ½   **cup chicken broth**
            Sliced almonds, toasted

1. Coat chicken pieces evenly with a mixture of
flour, salt, pepper, and rosemary.

2. Heat butter in a skillet. Add chicken pieces and brown evenly.
3. Put browned chicken into an electric cooker.
4. Put kumquats and syrup into an electric blender container; blend until smooth. Mix kumquat purée, ginger, and chicken broth with drippings in skillet. Heat to boiling. Pour sauce over chicken.
5. Cover and cook on Low 6 to 8 hours.
6. Garnish with almonds.

About 4 servings

Casa Chicken

 1 **broiler-fryer chicken (2 to 2½ pounds), cut in pieces**
 ¼ **teaspoon onion salt**
 ¼ **teaspoon pepper**
 ¼ **cup ketchup**
 2 **tablespoons soy sauce**
 1 **tablespoon prepared mustard**
 ¼ **teaspoon curry powder**
 1 **bay leaf**
 1 **cup water**

1. Put chicken pieces into an electric cooker. Sprinkle chicken evenly with onion salt and pepper.
2. Blend ketchup, soy sauce, mustard, curry powder, bay leaf, and water; pour over chicken.
3. Cover and cook on Low 8 to 10 hours.
4. Serve chicken on **hot fluffy rice** and spoon sauce over all.

About 4 servings

Chicken Slowpoke

 2 **carrots, pared and sliced**
 2 **stalks celery, sliced**
 2 **onions, peeled and sliced**
 1 **broiler-fryer chicken (2½ to 3 pounds), cut in pieces**
 2 **teaspoons salt**
 ¼ **teaspoon pepper**
 1 **teaspoon basil**
 ½ **cup hot canned chicken broth**

1. Layer vegetables in bottom of an electric cooker. Arrange chicken pieces on top. Sprinkle with seasonings and pour broth over all.
2. Cover and cook on Low 6 to 8 hours.

About 4 servings

Chicken à la King

 ¼ **cup finely chopped onion**
 ¼ **cup finely chopped celery**
 ¼ **cup finely chopped green pepper**
 ¼ **cup chopped pimento**
 1 **can (4 ounces) mushroom stems and pieces, drained**
 3 **cups diced cooked chicken or turkey**
 ½ **teaspoon seasoned salt**
 ⅛ **teaspoon pepper**
 1 **can (about 10 ounces) condensed cream of mushroom soup**
 1 **can (13 ounces) evaporated milk**

1. Put all ingredients into an electric cooker; mix.
2. Cover and cook on Low 2 to 3 hours, or until thoroughly heated; stir once.
3. Serve in **patty shells** or over **hot fluffy rice.**

About 6 servings

Roast Stuffed Turkey

 1 **turkey (6 to 8 pounds)**
 1 **package (7 ounces) herb-seasoned stuffing croutons**
 ½ **cup melted butter**
 ½ **cup hot water or chicken broth**
 2 **tablespoons butter**
 ½ **cup chopped celery**
 ½ **cup chopped onion**
 2 **tablespoons chopped parsley**
   Melted butter

1. Rinse turkey with cold water; pat dry.
2. Turn stuffing croutons into a bowl; add ½ cup melted butter and toss gently. Stir in hot water or broth.
3. Heat 2 tablespoons butter in a skillet. Add celery and onion; cook until tender. Add to bowl with stuffing; add parsley and toss to mix.
4. Spoon stuffing into cavities of bird. Place turkey, breast side up, in a large electric cooker. Insert a meat thermometer in inner thigh muscle. Brush with melted butter.
5. Cover and roast at 300°F until meat thermometer registers 180°–185°, about 6 hours.

6 to 10 servings

Note: If desired to enhance browning, place a piece of aluminum foil over turkey before covering with lid.

Barbecued Turkey Legs

4 small turkey legs (about 3 pounds)
½ cup flour
2 tablespoons fat
1 cup bottled barbecue sauce

1. Coat turkey legs with flour. Brown on all sides in hot fat in a large skillet.
2. Put browned turkey legs into an electric cooker. Pour in barbecue sauce.
3. Cover and cook on Low 8 to 10 hours.

4 servings

Shrimp Creole

¼ cup butter or margarine
1½ cups finely chopped onion
1½ cups finely chopped green pepper
2 cans (16 ounces each) tomatoes, sieved
2 teaspoons Worcestershire sauce
2 small bay leaves
1½ teaspoons salt
⅛ teaspoon pepper
1 teaspoon sugar
½ teaspoon oregano
2 pounds fresh shrimp, shelled and deveined

1. Heat butter in a skillet. Mix in onion and green pepper and cook until vegetables are partially tender. Turn mixture into an electric cooker. Add sieved tomatoes, Worcestershire sauce, bay leaves, salt, pepper, sugar, and oregano; stir.
2. Cover and cook on Low 4 to 6 hours.
3. Remove bay leaves. Stir in shrimp.
4. Cover and cook on High 1 hour.
5. Serve shrimp mixture on **hot fluffy rice.**

About 8 servings

Bouillabaisse

¼ cup olive oil
⅔ cup chopped onion
2 leeks, chopped (white part only)
1 clove garlic, crushed in a garlic press
2 small tomatoes, peeled and chopped
1 tablespoon minced parsley
½ bay leaf
¼ teaspoon savory
¼ teaspoon fennel
⅛ teaspoon saffron
1½ teaspoons salt
¼ teaspoon pepper
2 cups water
1½ pounds bass, cleaned and bones removed
1 pound perch, cleaned and bones removed
1 pound cod, cleaned and bones removed
1 lobster (1½ to 2 pounds), killed and cleaned
1 pound fresh shrimp, peeled and deveined
1 pint oysters, drained
6 slices French bread, toasted

1. Put olive oil, onion, leek, garlic, tomato, parsley, dry seasonings, and water into a large electric cooker; stir.
2. Cover and cook on High 2 to 4 hours.
3. Cut fish and lobster into 1½- to 2-inch pieces. Add to cooker; mix.
4. Cover and cook on High 2 hours.
5. Add shrimp and oysters; mix.
6. Cover and cook on High 1 hour.
7. Line a large, deep serving dish with toast; cover with seafood and sauce. Serve immediately.

6 to 8 servings

VEGETABLES

Pray how does your asparagus perform?
JOHN ADAMS, from a letter to Abigail

Asparagus in Ripe Olive Sauce

> 2 packages (10 ounces each) frozen asparagus
> ⅓ cup butter, melted
> ¼ cup ripe olive rings
> ½ clove garlic, minced
> 2 teaspoons lemon juice
> Dash each seasoned salt and pepper

1. Put asparagus into an electric cooker.
2. Cover and cook on High 1 hour, or until tender.
3. Add remaining ingredients and stir gently.
4. Cover and cook on Low 30 to 60 minutes.

About 6 servings

Creamy Green Beans

> 2 cans (16 ounces each) french-style green
>   beans, drained
> 1 can (about 10 ounces) cream of mushroom
>   soup
> ½ soup can hot water
> 1 can (3½ ounces) french-fried onion rings

1. Put green beans, soup, and water into an electric cooker; stir just to blend. Sprinkle onion rings over top.
2. Cover and cook on Low 4 hours.

6 to 8 servings

Old-fashioned Green Beans and Bacon

(A Pennsylvania Dutch specialty)

> 8 slices bacon, diced
> ¾ pound fresh green beans, cut in 2-inch
>   pieces
> 2 medium potatoes, pared and cut in ½-inch
>   pieces
> 1 small onion, peeled and sliced
> ¼ cup hot water
> ½ teaspoon salt

1. Fry bacon until crisp; reserve bacon and 1 tablespoon drippings.
2. Combine green beans, potatoes, onion, reserved bacon drippings, water, and salt in an electric cooker.
3. Cover and cook on High 3 to 4 hours, or until vegetables are tender.
4. Top vegetables with reserved bacon.

About 4 servings

Sweet-and-Sour Green Beans with Bananas

> 2 packages (9 ounces each) frozen
>   french-style green beans
> ½ teaspoon salt
> 1 tablespoon minced onion
> ¾ cup chicken broth (reserve ½ cup for sauce)
> 1 cup diced firm ripe bananas
> 2 tablespoons lemon juice
> 4 slices bacon
> 1 tablespoon flour
> 2 tablespoons vinegar
> 2 tablespoons sugar

1. Put beans, salt, onion, and ¼ cup chicken broth in electric cooker.
2. Toss bananas with lemon juice and add to cooker; mix gently.
3. Cover and cook on High 1½ to 2 hours.
4. Fry bacon until crisp in a skillet. Remove bacon from skillet and crumble; set aside.

5. Use 2 tablespoons of drippings in skillet and blend in flour; add reserved ½ cup chicken broth, vinegar, and sugar. Cook, stirring constantly, until mixture thickens and comes to boiling.

6. Transfer bean mixture to a serving dish and pour sauce over all. Toss gently to coat; sprinkle crumbled bacon over top.

4 to 6 servings

Green Beans with Water Chestnuts

> 1 pound fresh green beans, cut in ½-inch pieces
> 1 can (5 ounces) water chestnuts, drained and thinly sliced
> 3 tablespoons chopped onion
> ¾ teaspoon salt
> Few grains pepper
> 2 tablespoons lemon juice
> 2 cups hot water
> 1 teaspoon soy sauce

1. Combine beans, water chestnuts, onion, salt, pepper, lemon juice, and water in an electric cooker.

2. Cover and cook on High 4 hours, then on Low 8 to 10 hours.

3. Drain cooked bean mixture and toss with soy sauce.

4 to 6 servings

Beets in Orange Sauce

> 2 jars (16 ounces each) sliced beets, drained, reserving 1 cup liquid
> 1 small onion, grated
> 3 tablespoons sugar
> ½ teaspoon salt
> ⅛ teaspoon pepper
> 1 tablespoon cider vinegar
> 1 tablespoon butter or margarine
> 4 teaspoons grated orange peel
> ½ cup orange juice

1. Combine all ingredients in an electric cooker.

2. Cover and cook on High 1 hour.

3. Adjust seasonings, if necessary.

About 6 servings

Note: These beets could be refrigerated and served cold.

Broccoli with Horseradish Cream

> 2 packages (10 ounces each) frozen broccoli spears
> ½ cup boiling water
> ½ teaspoon salt
> ½ teaspoon prepared horseradish
> ½ teaspoon prepared mustard
> ¾ cup dairy sour cream

1. Put broccoli into an electric cooker; add water and salt.

2. Cover and cook on High 1 hour.

3. Combine horseradish, mustard, and sour cream; mix thoroughly.

4. Pour sauce over cooked broccoli.

5. Cover and cook on High 30 minutes.

4 to 6 servings

Total cooking time will be influenced by the temperature of foods when they go into the cooker. If you wish to cut overall time, heat the liquid the recipe calls for before it goes into the pot.

Red Cabbage, Danish Style

1 large head red cabbage
⅔ cup red currant syrup, or melted red currant jelly
⅓ cup butter, melted
6 tablespoons cider vinegar
6 tablespoons hot water
1 teaspoon sugar
½ teaspoon salt
2 large cooking apples, quartered, pared, cored, and sliced

1. Cut cabbage into quarters, cut out core, and remove tough outer leaves. Shred coarsely.
2. Put remaining ingredients into an electric cooker, add cabbage, and stir just to combine.
3. Cover and cook on High 3 to 4 hours.

About 8 servings

Company Cabbage

5 cups finely shredded cabbage
1 cup finely shredded carrot
½ cup chopped green onion
½ teaspoon salt
⅛ teaspoon pepper
1 cup hot chicken broth
  Boiling water
¼ cup butter or margarine
1 teaspoon prepared mustard
⅓ cup chopped pecans
¼ teaspoon paprika

1. Put cabbage, carrot, onion, salt, and pepper into an electric cooker. Pour in chicken broth and enough boiling water to cover vegetables.
2. Cover and cook on High 3 to 4 hours.
3. Melt butter in a small skillet; stir in mustard and pecans. Toss to coat.
4. Transfer vegetables to serving dish; top with butter-pecan mixture and sprinkle with paprika.

About 6 servings

Savory Brussels Sprouts

2 packages (10 ounces each) frozen Brussels sprouts
½ cup boiling water
⅛ teaspoon salt
⅓ cup butter, melted
1 tablespoon grated onion
1 tablespoon lemon juice
½ teaspoon salt
¼ teaspoon marjoram
¼ teaspoon savory
¼ teaspoon thyme

1. Put Brussels sprouts into an electric cooker; add water and salt.
2. Cover and cook on High 1 hour.
3. Combine butter, onion, lemon juice, and dry seasonings; mix thoroughly. Pour over cooked Brussels sprouts.
4. Cover and cook on High 30 minutes.

About 6 servings

Long cooking develops stronger flavor in many herbs and spices. Try cutting the amount in standard recipes by half.

Cooker Carrots

- **2 jars (16 ounces each) sliced carrots**
- **½ bunch green onions, finely chopped**
- **2 tablespoons butter or margarine, melted**
- **1 tablespoon sugar**
- **2 tablespoons honey**
- **¼ teaspoon salt**

1. Put carrots and onion into an electric cooker.
2. Mix butter, sugar, honey, and salt. Pour over vegetables.
3. Cover and cook on High 1 to 2 hours.

About 6 servings

Cauliflower with Cheese Sauce

- **1 large head cauliflower**
- **½ cup water**
- **1 teaspoon salt**
- **4 ounces Cheddar cheese, shredded**

1. Rinse cauliflower thoroughly in cold water and break into flowerets.
2. Put cauliflower into electric cooker; add water and salt.
3. Cover and cook on High 2 hours.
4. Drain off liquid from cauliflower; add cheese.
5. Cover and cook on High 15 minutes, or until cheese is completely melted.

4 to 6 servings

Stewed Celery and Tomatoes

- **3 pounds celery**
- **½ cup chopped onion**
- **2 tablespoons grated carrot**
- **2 tablespoons butter or margarine, melted**
- **3 tomatoes, peeled and cut in pieces**
- **1¼ teaspoons salt**
- **⅛ teaspoon pepper**
- **¼ teaspoon sugar**
- **¼ teaspoon crushed thyme**
- **1 vegetable bouillon cube**
- **2 tablespoons minced parsley**

1. Cut celery on the diagonal into 1-inch pieces.
2. Put celery and remaining ingredients into an electric cooker; stir just to combine.
3. Cover and cook on High 3 to 4 hours.

4 to 6 servings

Peas with Sweet Basil

- **1 package (10 ounces) frozen green peas, partially thawed**
- **½ cup sliced green onions with tops**
- **2 tablespoons melted butter or margarine**
- **1 tablespoon snipped parsley**
- **¼ cup hot water**
- **½ teaspoon sugar**
- **½ teaspoon salt**
- **¼ teaspoon sweet basil**
- **⅛ teaspoon pepper**

1. Combine all ingredients in electric cooker.
2. Cover and cook on High 1 hour, or until peas are tender.

About 4 servings

Scalloped Potatoes

    4 to 5 medium potatoes
    ¼ cup chopped onion
    2 tablespoons flour
    ¼ teaspoon salt
    2 tablespoons melted butter or margarine
    1 can (13 ounces) evaporated milk
    ⅓ cup water

1. Wash, pare, and thinly slice potatoes.
2. Layer potatoes and onion in an electric cooker; sprinkle each layer with flour and salt. Add melted butter, evaporated milk, and water.
3. Cover and cook on High 4 to 5 hours, or until potatoes are tender when pierced with fork.

About 6 servings

Dutch Stewed Potatoes

    2 cups diced raw potatoes
    1 onion, peeled and sliced
    1 tablespoon melted butter or other
        shortening
    1 teaspoon minced parsley
    1 teaspoon salt
      Few grains pepper
    ¾ cup boiling water
    1 tablespoon water
    2 teaspoons flour

1. Combine potatoes, onion, butter, parsley, salt, and pepper in electric cooker. Add boiling water; stir just to combine.
2. Cover and cook on High 3 to 4 hours, or until potatoes are tender.
3. Blend water and flour. Stir into mixture in cooker.
4. Cover and cook on High 30 minutes.

3 or 4 servings

Potatoes Anna

    6 to 8 medium potatoes
      Salt and pepper
    ½ cup butter or margarine, melted

1. Wash, pare, and cut potatoes into thin cross-wise slices. Dry thoroughly with absorbent paper.
2. Arrange even layers of potatoes in a buttered electric cooker, overlapping slices about ¼ inch.

Sprinkle each layer with salt and pepper and drizzle with melted butter.
3. Cover and cook on High 4 to 5 hours, or until potatoes are tender and browned at edges.

6 to 8 servings

Sauerkraut with Apples

    4 cups drained sauerkraut
    2 apples, thinly sliced
    ½ cup apple cider
    1 tablespoon light brown sugar
    2 tablespoons melted butter or margarine
      Apple wedges
      Parsley sprigs

1. Combine sauerkraut, sliced apples, apple cider, brown sugar, and butter in an electric cooker.
2. Cover and cook on High 3 to 4 hours, or until apples are tender.
3. Garnish with apple wedges and parsley.

About 8 servings

If you're running late, turn a cooker that has been on Low up to High. That will cut the remaining time in half.

Sauerkraut with Caraway

    2 cans (16 ounces each) sauerkraut
    1 potato, pared and grated
    ½ cup chopped onion
    2 tablespoons melted butter or margarine
    1 teaspoon caraway seed
    2 cups boiling water

1. Put all ingredients into an electric cooker; stir just to combine.
2. Cover and cook on High 3 to 4 hours.
3. If desired, 1 or 2 tablespoons of brown sugar may be stirred into mixture about 15 minutes before the end of cooking time.

6 to 8 servings

Spiced Spinach

- 1 pound fresh spinach
- ¼ cup butter or margarine, melted
- 1 clove garlic, minced
- 1 teaspoon lemon juice
- ½ to 1 teaspoon coriander
- ½ teaspoon salt
- ⅛ teaspoon seasoned pepper
- 1 hard-cooked egg, chopped

1. Wash and drain spinach; put into an electric cooker. Combine butter, garlic, lemon juice, and dry seasonings; pour over spinach. Toss to mix.
2. Cover and cook on High 1 hour, or until spinach is wilted but not soft.
3. Turn spinach into serving dish. Sprinkle with chopped egg. Serve immediately.

About 4 servings

Acorn Squash Stuffed with Corn

- 1 large acorn squash
- 2 cups canned whole kernel corn with peppers
- 2 tablespoons butter, softened
- ¼ teaspoon salt
- ⅛ teaspoon black pepper
- ¼ teaspoon basil, crushed

1. Cut acorn squash into quarters. Remove seedy centers.
2. Combine corn, butter, salt, pepper, and basil in a bowl.
3. Spoon corn filling into squash centers. Wrap each quarter in foil and place in an electric cooker.
4. Cover and cook on High 2 hours.

4 servings

Scalloped Sweet Potatoes and Apples

- 6 medium sweet potatoes, pared and cut in crosswise slices ¼ inch thick
- 1½ cups apple slices
- ½ cup firmly packed brown sugar
- ¼ cup butter or margarine, melted
- ½ cup apple juice
- 1 tablespoon lemon juice

1. Combine ingredients in an electric cooker.
2. Cover and cook on High 3 to 4 hours, or until sweet potatoes and apples are tender.

About 6 servings

Vegetable-Rice Medley

- 1½ pounds zucchini, thinly sliced
- 1 can (16 ounces) whole kernel corn, drained
- 1 can (16 ounces) tomatoes (undrained)
- ¾ cup chopped onion
- 3 tablespoons melted butter or margarine
- 1½ teaspoons salt
- ¼ teaspoon pepper
- ¼ teaspoon coriander
- ¼ teaspoon oregano leaves
- 3 cups cooked white rice

1. Put all ingredients, except rice, into electric cooker; stir just to combine.
2. Cover and cook on High 1 to 2 hours, or until zucchini is tender.
3. Add cooked rice and stir gently.
4. Cover and cook on High 15 minutes.

About 8 servings

Creamy Molasses Limas

1 pound dried baby lima beans, rinsed
½ cup firmly packed brown sugar
1 teaspoon salt
¼ cup butter, melted
¼ cup dark molasses
2 tablespoons prepared mustard
½ cup water
1 cup dairy sour cream

1. Put beans into a large saucepan. Add 1½ quarts water. Cover and let stand overnight.
2. The next day, drain beans and put into an electric cooker. Add remaining ingredients, except sour cream, and mix thoroughly.
3. Cover and cook on High 6 to 8 hours.
4. Mix sour cream with beans before serving.

6 to 8 servings

Easy Black-eye Peas

1 pound dried black-eye peas, rinsed
1 quart water
½ pound salt pork, slab bacon, or smoked ham
1 teaspoon sugar
1 teaspoon salt
Few grains pepper

1. Soak beans either by overnight method or quick method. *Overnight method:* Cover beans with 1 quart water; add ¼ teaspoon baking soda if water is hard. *Quick method:* Bring 1 quart water to boiling in a saucepan; add rinsed beans and cook 2 minutes only. Cover; remove from heat. Allow to stand for 1 hour.
2. Transfer beans and soaking liquid to an electric cooker. Add remaining ingredients.
3. Cover and cook on High 3 to 4 hours.

6 to 8 servings

Vegetable Goulash

1 can (about 15 ounces) kidney beans (undrained)
1½ cups fresh corn kernels (cut from about 3 ears)
1 cup chopped celery
1 cup chopped onion
½ cup chopped green pepper
1 can (8 ounces) tomato sauce
1 teaspoon brown sugar
½ to ¾ teaspoon chili powder
⅛ teaspoon pepper

1. Combine all ingredients in an electric cooker.
2. Cover and cook on High 4 hours, or until vegetables are tender.

6 to 8 servings

Crockery Lima Beans

1 pound dried large lima beans, rinsed
5 slices bacon
Butter
1 large onion, peeled and chopped
2 tablespoons flour
1 can (16 ounces) tomatoes (undrained)
1 teaspoon salt
¼ teaspoon pepper

1. Put beans into a large saucepot or Dutch oven. Add 1½ quarts water. Cover and let stand overnight.
2. Fry bacon in a skillet until partially cooked. Remove from skillet, drain and crumble.
3. Measure bacon drippings and add butter to make ⅓ cup. Put fat into skillet, add onion, and cook until golden. Stir in flour.
4. Drain beans and put into an electric cooker. Add onion mixture, tomatoes, salt, pepper, and bacon; stir.
5. Cover and cook on Low 12 to 14 hours.

About 6 servings

BREADS

Could we have some butter
for the Royal slice of bread?

A. A. MILNE, *The King's Breakfast*

Cranberry Fruit-Nut Bread

    2   cups all-purpose flour
    1   cup sugar
    1½ teaspoons baking powder
    1   teaspoon salt
    ½   teaspoon baking soda
    1¼ cups cranberries, cut in halves
    ½   cup walnuts, coarsely chopped
    1   egg, well beaten
    1   teaspoon grated orange peel
    ¾   cup orange juice
    2   tablespoons melted butter or margarine

1. Mix flour with sugar, baking powder, salt, and baking soda in a bowl. Mix in cranberries and walnuts.
2. Blend egg, orange peel and juice, and butter in a bowl. Make a well in center of dry ingredients; add liquid mixture and stir only enough to moisten dry ingredients.
3. Turn into a well-greased and floured cooker bake pan or 2-pound coffee can. Cover bake pan with lid; or, if using coffee can, cover with 6 layers of paper toweling. Set in an electric cooker.
4. Cover and cook on High 3 to 4 hours.
5. Remove bake pan and let cool 10 minutes before removing bread.

1 loaf bread

Irish Soda Bread with Currants

    2   cups all-purpose flour
    1   tablespoon sugar
    1   teaspoon baking soda
    ¾   teaspoon salt
    2   tablespoons butter or margarine
    ⅓   cup dried currants, rinsed
    ¼   cup white vinegar
    ½   cup milk

1. Mix flour with sugar, baking soda, and salt in a bowl. Cut in butter with pastry blender or two knives until particles resemble rice kernels. Lightly mix in currants.
2. Mix vinegar and milk. Add half of the liquid to dry ingredients; blend quickly. Add remaining liquid and stir only until blended.
3. Turn dough onto floured surface. Lightly knead dough about 10 times. Shape dough into a ball; put into a well-greased and floured 2-pound coffee

can. If desired, cut a shallow cross in center of loaf. Cover can with 6 layers of paper toweling. Set in an electric cooker.
4. Cover and cook on High 2 hours, or until a wooden pick inserted in bread comes out clean.
5. Remove can and unmold bread. Serve warm.

1 loaf bread

Oatmeal-Raisin Bread

    2   cups all-purpose flour
    ½   cup sugar
    1   tablespoon baking powder
    1½ teaspoons salt
    1   teaspoon cinnamon
    ½   teaspoon baking soda
    ¼   teaspoon mace or nutmeg
    1   cup uncooked oats
    1   cup (about 5 ounces) raisins
    ½   cup (about 2 ounces) chopped nuts
    1¼ cups sour milk (see Note, page 81)
    ¼   cup firmly packed brown sugar
    1   egg, well beaten
    3   tablespoons shortening, melted and cooled

1. Mix flour with sugar, baking powder, cinnamon, salt, baking soda, and mace. Stir in oats, raisins, and nuts. Make a well in the center and set aside.
2. Mix sour milk, brown sugar, egg, and melted shortening. Add to dry ingredients all at one time; stir only enough to moisten dry ingredients.
3. Turn into a well-greased and floured cooker bake pan or 2-pound coffee can. Cover bake pan

with lid; or, if using coffee can, cover with 6 layers of paper toweling. Set in an electric cooker.
4. Cover and cook on High 2 to 3 hours.
5. Remove bake pan and let cool 10 minutes before removing bread.

1 loaf bread

Apricot-Nut Bread

½ cup diced dried apricots
1 egg
1 cup sugar
2 tablespoons melted butter
2 cups all-purpose flour
1 tablespoon baking powder
¾ teaspoon salt
¼ teaspoon baking soda
½ cup orange juice
¼ cup water
1 cup broken walnut pieces

1. Soak and drain apricots. Finely slice or grind; set aside.
2. Beat egg until light and fluffy. Stir in sugar and butter; mix well.
3. Mix flour with baking powder, salt, and baking soda. Add dry ingredients alternately in thirds with orange juice and water in halves to the creamed mixture, mixing well after each addition.
4. Add apricots and nuts; mix. Turn into well-greased and floured cooker bake pan or 2-pound coffee can. Cover bake pan with lid; or, if using coffee can, cover with 6 layers of paper toweling. Set pan in an electric cooker.
5. Cover and cook on High 3 to 4 hours.
6. Remove bake pan and let cool 10 minutes before removing bread.

1 loaf bread

Gingerbread

1½ cups all-purpose flour
½ teaspoon baking soda
⅛ teaspoon salt
1 teaspoon cinnamon
1 teaspoon ginger
½ teaspoon cloves
⅛ teaspoon nutmeg
¼ cup butter or margarine
½ cup sugar
1 egg
½ cup light molasses
2 tablespoons hot water
½ cup sour milk (see Note)

1. Mix flour with baking soda, salt, and spices; set aside.
2. Cream butter with sugar. Add egg and beat thoroughly.
3. Combine molasses and hot water; add gradually to creamed mixture, blending well.
4. Alternately add dry ingredients in thirds and sour milk in halves to creamed mixture, beating only until smooth after each addition.
5. Turn into a well-greased and floured 2-pound coffee can. Cover can with 6 layers of paper toweling. Set in an electric cooker.
6. Cover and cook on High 2 to 3 hours.
7. Remove bake pan and let cool 10 minutes before removing bread.

1 loaf bread

Note: For ½ cup sour milk, measure 1½ teaspoons vinegar into liquid measuring cup and fill with milk to the ½-cup level; stir.

Nutty Orange-Date Bread

2 cups all-purpose flour
1 teaspoon baking powder
1 teaspoon baking soda
½ teaspoon salt
1 teaspoon orange peel
1 cup orange juice
¼ cup butter or margarine
1 cup sugar
1 egg
1 cup pitted dates, chopped
½ cup chopped pecans

1. Mix flour with baking powder, baking soda, and salt; set aside.
2. Combine orange peel with orange juice; set aside.
3. Cream butter with sugar. Add egg and beat until light and fluffy.
4. Alternately add dry ingredients in thirds and orange juice in halves to egg mixture, beating until well blended after each addition. Mix in dates and pecans.
5. Turn into a well-greased and floured cooker bake pan or 2-pound coffee can. Cover bake pan with lid; or, if using coffee can, cover with 6 layers of paper toweling. Set in an electric cooker.
6. Cover and cook on High 2 to 3 hours.
7. Remove bake pan and let cool 10 minutes before removing bread.

1 loaf bread

Lemon-Saffron Bread

1½ cups all-purpose flour
1½ teaspoons baking powder
¼ teaspoon baking soda
¼ teaspoon salt
    Pinch powdered Spanish saffron
¼ cup hot water
1 tablespoon grated lemon peel
¼ cup lemon juice
¼ cup shortening
½ cup sugar
1 egg

1. Mix flour with baking powder, baking soda, and salt.
2. Dissolve saffron in hot water; blend with lemon peel and juice. Set aside.
3. Cream shortening; add sugar gradually, beating until thoroughly blended. Add egg and beat until light and fluffy.
4. Add dry ingredients in fourths and liquid in thirds, mixing just until blended after each addition.
5. Turn into a well-greased and floured cooker bake pan or 2-pound coffee can. Cover bake pan with lid; or, if using coffee can, cover with 6 layers of paper toweling. Set in an electric cooker.
6. Cover and cook on High 2 to 3 hours.
7. Remove bake pan and let cool 10 minutes before removing bread.

1 loaf bread

Spoonbread

2 eggs
2 cups milk
2 tablespoons melted butter or margarine
1 cup cornmeal
1 teaspoon baking powder
1 teaspoon sugar
½ teaspoon salt

1. Beat eggs until light and foamy in a bowl. Add milk and butter. Mix remaining ingredients and stir into egg mixture.
2. Turn into a well-greased and floured 2-pound coffee can. Cover coffee can with 6 layers of paper toweling. Set in an electric cooker.
3. Cover and cook on High 2 to 3 hours, or until bread tests done in center.
4. Remove coffee can and serve spoonbread hot.

About 6 servings

Boston Brown Bread

⅔ cup rye flour
⅔ cup whole wheat flour
⅔ cup yellow cornmeal
1 teaspoon baking powder
¾ teaspoon salt
½ teaspoon baking soda
1⅓ cups buttermilk or sour milk (see Note, page 81)
⅔ cup dark seedless raisins
½ cup molasses

1. Mix flours with cornmeal, baking powder, salt, and baking soda in a large bowl. Mix buttermilk, molasses, and raisins; add to dry ingredients and stir only enough to moisten the flour.
2. Pour batter into a well-greased and floured 2-pound coffee can. Cover with foil; tie. Set in an electric cooker. Pour 2 cups hot water around can.
3. Cover and cook on High 2 to 3 hours.
4. Remove coffee can and let cool 1 hour before unmolding bread.

1 loaf bread

Cheerie Cherry Bread

1½ cups all-purpose flour
1½ teaspoons baking powder
¼ teaspoon salt
2 eggs
¾ cup sugar
1 bottle (6 ounces) maraschino cherries, drained (reserve ⅓ cup syrup) and cut in pieces (about ½ cup)
¾ cup pecans, coarsely chopped

1. Mix flour with baking powder and salt.
2. Beat eggs and sugar together until thick and piled softly.
3. Alternately add dry ingredients in thirds and reserved cherry syrup in halves to egg mixture, mixing until well blended after each addition. Mix in cherries and pecans.
4. Turn into a well-greased and floured cooker bake pan or 2-pound coffee can. Cover bake pan with lid; or, if using coffee can, cover with 6 layers of paper toweling. Set in an electric cooker.
5. Cover and cook on High for 2 to 3 hours.
6. Remove bake pan and let cool 10 minutes before removing bread.

1 loaf bread

DESSERTS

Married ladies who love your lords, give them puddings.

JOSEPH BARBER, *Crumbs from the Round Table*

California Orange-Date Cake

- ⅓ cup shortening
- ¾ teaspoon grated orange peel
- ½ teaspoon grated lemon peel
- 1 cup sugar
- 2 eggs
- 1½ cups all-purpose flour
- ¾ teaspoon baking powder
- ½ teaspoon baking soda
- ⅛ teaspoon salt
- ⅔ cup buttermilk
- ¼ cup orange juice
- 1 package (8 ounces) pitted dates, finely snipped
- ⅔ cup finely chopped pecans
- ½ cup orange juice
- ⅓ cup sugar

1. Cream shortening, orange peel, and lemon peel; gradually add 1 cup sugar, beating until fluffy. Add eggs, one at a time, beating well after each addition.
2. Mix flour, baking powder, soda, and salt. Add to creamed mixture alternately with buttermilk and ¼ cup orange juice, beating only until smooth after each addition. Stir in dates and pecans.
3. Pour batter into a greased and floured cooker bake pan or a 2-pound coffee can. Cover bake pan with lid; or, if using a coffee can, cover with 6 layers of paper toweling. Set pan in an electric cooker.
4. Cover and cook on High 2 to 3 hours.
5. Remove cake from pan to serving plate.
6. Combine remaining juice and sugar in a small saucepan; set over low heat and stir until sugar dissolves. Spoon syrup over cake. If desired, serve with sweetened whipped cream.

About 8 servings

Vanilla Wafer Cake

- ¾ cup butter or margarine
- 1½ cups sugar
- 4 eggs
- 1 package (7¼ ounces) vanilla wafers
- ¼ cup plus 2 tablespoons milk
- ¾ cup flaked coconut
- ¾ cup chopped pecans

1. Cream butter and sugar. Add eggs, one at a time, beating well after each addition.
2. Finely crush vanilla wafers; add to creamed mixture along with milk, coconut, and pecans; mix well.
3. Turn batter into a well-greased and floured 2-pound coffee can. Cover can with 6 layers of paper toweling. Set pan in an electric cooker.
4. Cover and cook on High 3 to 4 hours. Cooker lid should be slightly raised during cooking to allow release of excess moisture.

8 to 10 servings

Crockery Wallbanger Cake

- 1 package (15 ounces) pound cake mix
- 1 package (3½ ounces) lemon instant pudding and pie filling mix
- ½ cup vegetable oil
- ½ cup orange juice
- ¼ cup anise-flavored liqueur, such as Galliano
- 4 eggs
  Glaze (see below)

1. Blend cake mix, pudding mix, oil, orange juice, liqueur, and eggs. Beat on medium speed of an electric mixer 30 seconds; scrape beaters and bowl; beat 2 minutes longer.
2. Pour into well-greased and floured cooker bake pan or 1-pound coffee can.
3. Cover bake pan with lid, or, if using coffee can, cover with 6 layers of paper toweling. Set pan in an electric cooker.
4. Cover cooker and cook on High 2½ hours, or until cake springs back when lightly touched.

5. Cool cake in pan 5 minutes; loosen edges with knife and invert on serving plate. While still warm, poke holes in cake with a skewer and pour glaze over all.

About 8 servings

Glaze: Combine ½ **cup confectioners' sugar** and **1 tablespoon anise-flavored liqueur.**

Applesauce Cake

   2 **cups all-purpose flour**
   1 **teaspoon baking soda**
   1 **teaspoon cinnamon**
  ½ **teaspoon cloves**
  ½ **teaspoon nutmeg**
  ¼ **teaspoon salt**
  ½ **cup butter**
   1 **cup firmly packed light brown sugar**
   1 **cup unsweetened applesauce**
   1 **cup raisins**

1. Mix flour, baking soda, cinnamon, cloves, nutmeg, and salt.
2. Beat butter until softened. Add brown sugar gradually, creaming until fluffy. Alternately add the dry ingredients in fourths and applesauce in thirds to creamed mixture, mixing until blended after each addition. Mix in raisins.
3. Turn batter into a greased and floured cooker bake pan. Cover with lid. Set pan in an electric cooker.
4. Cover and cook on High 3 to 4 hours, or until cake tester or wooden pick comes out clean when inserted in center, or top springs back when lightly touched.

6 to 8 servings

Super Turban Cake

 2¼ **cups sifted all-purpose flour**
 2¼ **teaspoons baking powder**
  ½ **cup butter**
   1 **tablespoon grated lemon peel**
   1 **teaspoon vanilla extract**
  ½ **cup sugar**
   4 **egg yolks (⅓ cup), well beaten**
  ¾ **cup milk**
   4 **egg whites (½ cup)**
  ½ **cup sugar**
      Chocolate Glaze (see below)

1. Sift the flour and baking powder together; set aside.
2. Cream butter with lemon peel and vanilla extract. Add ½ cup sugar gradually, creaming until fluffy after each addition. Add the beaten egg yolks in thirds, beating well after each addition.
3. Beating only until smooth after each addition, alternately add dry ingredients in thirds and milk in halves to creamed mixture.
4. Beat the egg whites until frothy. Add ½ cup sugar gradually, beating well after each addition; beat until stiff peaks are formed. Gently fold into batter. Turn into a greased and floured 12-cup fluted tube pan. Top with 6 layers of paper toweling.
5. Put pan into a large electric cooker.
6. Cover and cook on High 2½ to 3½ hours, or until cake tester inserted in center comes out clean.
7. Cool cake on wire rack. Loosen cake from pan by running a small spatula carefully around the tube and edge of cake. Spread warm Chocolate Glaze over the cake. Allow 2 to 3 hours for glaze to set.

8 to 10 servings

Chocolate Glaze: Melt **4 ounces semisweet chocolate pieces** in a heavy saucepan over low heat. Remove from heat and stir in ¼ **cup butter** until blended.

Apple Cake

  ½ **cup vegetable oil**
   1 **cup sugar**
   2 **eggs**
  ½ **teaspoon vanilla extract**
 1½ **cups all-purpose flour**
  ¾ **teaspoon baking soda**
  ½ **teaspoon salt**
  ½ **teaspoon cinnamon**
  ¼ **teaspoon nutmeg**
  ¼ **teaspoon cloves**
 1½ **cups diced pared apples**
  ½ **cup chopped pecans**

1. Combine oil, sugar, eggs, vanilla extract, flour, baking soda, salt, and spices; mix thoroughly.
2. Mix in apples and pecans.
3. Turn batter into a greased and floured cooker bake pan or 2-pound coffee can. Cover bake pan with lid; or, if using coffee can, cover with 6 layers of paper toweling. Set pan in an electric cooker.
4. Cover and cook on High 3 to 4 hours.
5. Set pan on wire rack to cool.

8 to 10 servings

Nut Pound Cake

    1 cup butter or margarine
    1 cup sugar
    3 eggs
    1 teaspoon vanilla extract
    2 cups all-purpose flour
 1½ teaspoons baking powder
    ¼ teaspoon salt
 1½ cups chopped walnuts

1. Cream together butter and sugar. Add eggs, one at a time, beating well after each addition. Mix in vanilla extract.
2. Stir flour, baking powder, and salt together; add to creamed mixture and mix thoroughly. Stir in nuts.
3. Turn into a well-greased and floured cooker bake pan or 2-pound coffee can. Cover bake pan with lid; or, if using coffee can, cover with 6 layers of paper toweling. Set in an electric cooker.
4. Cover and cook on High 2 to 3 hours, or until cake tests done in the center. Cooker lid should be slightly raised during cooking to allow release of excess moisture.

1 pound cake

Flowerpot Banana Cake

    ½ cup butter or margarine
    1 cup sugar
    2 eggs
    1 cup mashed, quite ripe bananas
    2 cups all-purpose flour
    1 teaspoon baking soda
    ½ teaspoon salt
    ⅓ cup milk
    1 teaspoon lemon juice
    ½ cup chopped walnuts

1. Grease three 3½-inch flowerpots; line with waxed paper and grease the paper.
2. Cream butter and sugar; beat in eggs and bananas.
3. Mix flour with baking soda and salt; combine milk and lemon juice. Add dry ingredients alternately with milk to creamed mixture, mixing after each addition. Stir in nuts.
4. Pour batter into lined flowerpots.
5. Put flowerpots into a large electric cooker. Place 2 or 3 layers of paper toweling over flowerpots.
6. Cover and cook on High 1½ to 2 hours.

3 loaves banana cake

Crockery Fruitcake

    ¾ cup (about 4½ ounces) snipped dried figs
    ½ cup (about 3 ounces) snipped pitted dates
    ½ cup (about 2½ ounces) dark seedless raisins
    ½ cup (about 2½ ounces) golden raisins
    ½ cup (about 2½ ounces) diced candied citron
    ½ cup (about 2½ ounces) diced candied lemon peel
    ½ cup (about 2½ ounces) diced candied orange peel
    ¼ cup (about 1½ ounces) diced candied pineapple
    ¼ cup (about 1½ ounces) halved red candied cherries
    ¼ cup (about 1 ounce) currants
    ¼ cup sherry
    ¼ cup orange juice
    ½ cup (about 2 ounces) pecan halves
    2 cups all-purpose flour
    1 teaspoon baking powder
    ¼ teaspoon salt
    ½ teaspoon cinnamon
    ¼ teaspoon nutmeg
    ½ cup butter or margarine
    ½ teaspoon orange extract
    1 cup sugar
    3 eggs

1. Combine fruit, sherry, and orange juice in a large bowl. Cover tightly and set aside for 24 hours; stir occasionally.

2. Add nuts to fruit. Mix flour, baking powder, salt, cinnamon, and nutmeg; add to fruit and nuts; toss until pieces are well coated.

3. Cream butter with extract and sugar in a bowl; beat until light and fluffy. Add eggs, one at a time, beating thoroughly after each addition. (Mixture may be slightly curdled, but this will not affect the final product.) Using a spoon, thoroughly combine the creamed and fruit-nut mixtures.

4. Spoon batter into a greased and floured 2-pound coffee can. If desired, top with candied fruit and/or blanched almonds. Cover with 6 layers of paper toweling. Set can in an electric cooker.

5. Cover and cook on High 4 to 5 hours. Cooker lid should be slightly raised during cooking to allow release of excess moisture.

6. Set can on wire rack to cool.

One 3-pound fruitcake

Steamed Date Pudding

  1¾ **cups all-purpose flour**
  2 **teaspoons baking powder**
  1 **teaspoon salt**
  ½ **teaspoon cinnamon**
  1 **cup finely snipped dates**
  1 **cup chopped walnuts**
  ⅔ **cup butter or margarine**
  1 **cup firmly packed dark brown sugar**
  2 **eggs**
  ⅔ **cup undiluted evaporated milk**
  ⅓ **cup water**
     Hard Sauce (see below)

1. Mix 1½ cups flour with baking powder, salt, and cinnamon. Mix remaining ¼ cup flour with dates and walnuts to coat well.

2. Cream butter and brown sugar until light and fluffy. Add eggs, one at a time, beating well after each addition. Combine milk and water; add alternately with dry ingredients to creamed mixture, beginning and ending with dry ingredients. Add date-nut mixture; mix until well blended.

3. Turn into a greased and floured 2-pound coffee can and cover with 4 to 6 layers of paper toweling. Set can in an electric cooker. Pour 1½ cups boiling water around can.

4. Cover and cook on High 2 to 4 hours.

5. Unmold and serve hot with Hard Sauce.

About 6 servings

Hard Sauce: Cream ⅔ cup butter or margarine with **2 teaspoons vanilla extract**. Add **2 cups confectioners' sugar** with **few grains salt** gradually, beating until fluffy after each addition. Beat in **2 teaspoons cream**. If desired, press hard sauce evenly into an 8-inch square pan. Chill until firm and cut into squares or fancy shapes.

Bishop's Cake

  1½ **cups all-purpose flour**
  1 **teaspoon baking powder**
  ½ **teaspoon salt**
  3 **eggs**
  ¾ **cup sugar**
  1 **cup (about 7 ounces) small date pieces**
  1 **cup (about 8 ounces) maraschino cherries, drained and sliced**
  2 **cup walnuts, coarsely chopped**
  1 **package (6 ounces) semisweet chocolate pieces**

1. Mix flour with baking powder and salt.

2. Beat the eggs and sugar together until mixture is thick and piled softly.

3. Add dry ingredients in halves to egg mixture, beating only until blended after each addition. Stir in fruits, nuts, and chocolate pieces.

4. Turn into well-greased and floured cooker bake pan or 2-pound coffee can. Cover bake pan with lid; or, if using coffee can, cover with 6 layers of paper toweling. Set in an electric cooker.

5. Cover electric cooker and cook on High for 2 to 3 hours.

6. Remove bake pan and let cool 10 minutes before removing cake.

1 loaf cake

Chocolate Nut Pudding

Batter:
- 1 cup all-purpose biscuit mix
- ⅓ cup sugar
- 2 tablespoons cocoa
- ⅓ cup milk
- 1 teaspoon vanilla extract
- ½ cup chopped nuts

Topping:
- ½ cup lightly packed brown sugar
- 3 tablespoons cocoa
- ¾ cup boiling water

1. For batter, combine biscuit mix, sugar, and cocoa, stirring until well blended.
2. Add milk and vanilla extract, stirring only until batter is smooth; do not overmix. Stir in nuts.
3. Turn batter into well-greased cooker bake pan or 1-pound coffee can (or use a 2-pound can if cooker lid will fit tightly over top when can is inside).
4. For topping, stir brown sugar and cocoa together until smooth. Add boiling water gradually, stirring until sugar is dissolved. Pour onto batter.
5. Put lid on cooker pan; or if using coffee can, cover with 6 layers of paper towels. Set pan in electric cooker.
6. Cover and cook on High 2½ hours.
7. At serving time, carefully unmold pudding onto a serving dish with sides.
8. Serve pudding warm with whipped topping, if desired.

4 servings

Steamed Pumpkin Pudding

- 1¼ cups fine dry bread crumbs
- ½ cup all-purpose flour
- 1 cup lightly packed brown sugar
- 1 teaspoon baking powder
- ½ teaspoon baking soda
- ½ teaspoon salt
- ½ teaspoon cinnamon
- ½ teaspoon cloves
- 2 eggs, fork beaten
- 1½ cups canned pumpkin
- ½ cup vegetable oil
- ½ cup undiluted evaporated milk
- Lemon Zest Crème (see below)

1. Combine bread crumbs, flour, brown sugar, baking powder, baking soda, salt, cinnamon, and cloves in a large bowl. Set aside.
2. Beat eggs and remaining ingredients together. Add to dry ingredients; mix until blended.
3. Turn into a well-greased and floured 2-pound coffee can. Top with 4 to 6 layers of paper toweling. Place coffee can in electric cooker. Pour 1½ cups hot water around can.
4. Cover and cook on High 3 to 4 hours.
5. Unmold pudding onto serving plate and accompany with Lemon Zest Crème.

About 6 servings

Lemon Zest Crème: Cream ½ cup butter with ½ teaspoon ginger and ¼ teaspoon salt in a bowl. Add 2 cups confectioners' sugar gradually, beating constantly. Add 3 tablespoons lemon juice gradually, continuing to beat until well blended. Mix in ½ cup chopped nuts.

2½ cups sauce

Plum Pudding

- 1 cup all-purpose flour
- 1 teaspoon baking soda
- ½ teaspoon salt
- 2 teaspoons cinnamon
- ½ to 1 teaspoon cloves
- 1 teaspoon mace
- 4 ounces suet, finely chopped (about 1 cup)
- 1 cup sugar
- 2 cups soft bread crumbs
- 2 eggs, well beaten
- ¼ cup orange juice
- 1 cup milk
- 1 cup dark seedless raisins
- 1 cup currants
- ½ cup nuts, chopped
- ¼ cup finely chopped candied orange peel
- ¼ cup finely chopped candied lemon peel

1. Mix flour, baking soda, salt, and spices. Set aside.
2. Combine suet with sugar, bread crumbs, and eggs; beat together. Mix in orange juice.
3. Alternately add the dry ingredients in thirds and the milk in halves to the suet mixture, mixing well after each addition. Mix in raisins, currants, nuts, and peels.
4. Turn batter into a well-greased and floured 2-pound coffee can. Cover with foil; tie with string. Set can in an electric cooker. Pour 1½ cups boiling water around can.
5. Cover and cook on High 4 to 6 hours.
6. Unmold and serve hot with **Hard Sauce** (page 87).

About 12 servings

constantly. Continue to stir, bring to boiling, and simmer 5 minutes. Remove from heat and blend in **¼ cup butter** and **2 teaspoons vanilla extract.** Serve warm.

Steamed Raisin Pudding

- **1½ cups all-purpose flour**
- **½ teaspoon baking soda**
- **½ teaspoon salt**
- **¼ teaspoon allspice**
- **¼ teaspoon cinnamon**
- **¼ teaspoon nutmeg**
- **⅛ teaspoon cloves**
- **2 ounces suet, finely chopped (about ½ cup)**
- **½ cup molasses**
- **½ cup milk**
- **2 tablespoons water**
- **½ cup dark seedless raisins**
  Brown Sugar Pudding Sauce (see below)

1. Mix flour, baking soda, salt, and spices.
2. Combine suet with molasses, milk, and water. Stir in the dry ingredients, then raisins.
3. Turn mixture into a well-greased and floured 2-pound coffee can. Cover with 4 to 6 layers of paper toweling. Set in an electric cooker. Pour 1½ cups boiling water around can.
4. Cover and cook on High 3 to 4 hours.
5. Serve with the sauce.

About 12 servings

Brown Sugar Pudding Sauce: Combine **1 egg**, well beaten, **1 cup packed brown sugar**, and **1 teaspoon vanilla extract**; beat until creamy.

Orange Marmalade Pudding

- **1 cup butter or margarine**
- **1 cup sugar**
- **4 eggs, well beaten**
- **1 cup orange marmalade**
- **1 cup all-purpose flour**
- **1 teaspoon baking soda**

1. Beat butter until softened. Add sugar gradually, creaming thoroughly. Add eggs in thirds, beating thoroughly after each addition, until mixture is light and fluffy. Beat in marmalade.
2. Mix flour and baking soda thoroughly and add to butter mixture in fourths, beating only until blended after each addition.
3. Pour batter into a greased cooker bake pan. Cover with lid. Set pan in an electric cooker. Pour 1½ cups boiling water around pan.
4. Cover and cook on High 3 to 4 hours.
5. Spoon pudding into serving dishes and serve with Vanilla Sauce.

About 8 servings

Vanilla Sauce: Blend **1 cup sugar, 2 tablespoons cornstarch,** and **¼ teaspoon salt** in a saucepan. Add **2 cups boiling water** gradually, stirring

Bread Pudding

- **½ cup sugar**
- **¼ teaspoon nutmeg**
- **2 cups milk**
- **2 eggs, well beaten**
- **4 cups ½-inch slightly dry bread or cake cubes**
- **¼ cup raisins**

1. Add sugar, nutmeg, and milk to eggs; beat well.
2. Put bread cubes into a buttered electric cooker and pour egg mixture over bread. Allow to stand until bread is thoroughly soaked. Mix in the raisins.
3. Cover and cook on High 2 to 3 hours.

4 to 6 servings

Steamed Carrot Pudding

- 1 cup all-purpose flour
- 1 cup firmly packed brown sugar
- 1 teaspoon baking soda
- ¼ teaspoon salt
- 1 teaspoon cinnamon
- ½ teaspoon allspice
- ¼ teaspoon nutmeg
- ⅓ cup butter or margarine
- 1 egg
- 1 cup grated carrots
- 1 cup grated apples
- ½ cup golden raisins

1. Combine flour, brown sugar, baking soda, salt, and spices in a bowl. Make a well in center.
2. Cream butter and egg together. Turn into well in dry ingredients and mix until smooth.
3. Stir in carrots, apples, and raisins.
4. Turn into a well-greased and floured cooker bake pan or 2-pound coffee can. Cover bake pan with lid; or, if using coffee can, cover with 6 layers of paper toweling. Set pan in an electric cooker and pour 1½ cups boiling water around can.
5. Cover and cook on High 4 to 5 hours, or until cake tests done in the center.
6. If desired, serve with Hard Sauce (page 87).

About 8 servings

3. Beating just until blended after each addition, alternately add the dry ingredients in fourths and milk in thirds. Stir in the almonds.
4. Turn batter into a buttered 2-pound coffee can. Cover with 4 to 6 layers of paper toweling. Set can in an electric cooker. Pour 1½ cups boiling water around can.
5. Cover and cook on High 2 to 4 hours.
6. Serve warm with Hard Sauce (page 87).

6 to 8 servings

Steamed Chocolate Pudding

- 1⅓ cups all-purpose flour
- 1½ teaspoons baking powder
- ½ teaspoon salt
- ⅔ cup butter or margarine
- 2 teaspoons vanilla extract
- ¾ cup plus 2 tablespoons sugar
- 2 eggs
- 3 ounces (3 squares) unsweetened chocolate, melted and cooled
- ¾ cup milk
- 1 cup unblanched almonds, toasted and coarsely chopped

1. Mix flour, baking powder, and salt.
2. Cream butter with extract until softened; add sugar gradually, beating constantly until blended. Beat in eggs, one at a time, until mixture is fluffy. Blend in chocolate.

Apple-Cheese Betty

- 3 cups coarse bread crumbs
- 1½ cups shredded sharp Cheddar cheese (about 6 ounces)
- ¾ cup sugar
- 1 teaspoon cinnamon
- 6 apples, pared, cored, and sliced
- ¼ cup cold water

1. Combine bread crumbs and cheese. Mix sugar and cinnamon.
2. Arrange layers of apples, sugar mixture, and crumb mixture in a buttered cooker bake pan, making 3 layers of each. Drizzle water over last sugar mixture and top with last crumb mixture. Cover bake pan with lid. Set pan in an electric cooker.
3. Cover and cook on High 3 to 4 hours.

About 6 servings

Apple-Lemon Brown Betty

- **4** cups small bread cubes
- **¾** cup firmly packed brown sugar
- **2** teaspoons fresh grated lemon peel
- **2** tablespoons fresh lemon juice
- **¾** teaspoon cinnamon
- **⅛** teaspoon salt
- **4** cups chopped apple
- **½** cup butter or margarine, melted

1. Thoroughly mix bread cubes, brown sugar, lemon peel and juice, cinnamon, and salt.
2. Butter a 1-pound coffee can and layer chopped apple and crumb mixture, ending with crumbs. Pour melted butter over all, and place 2 or 3 paper towels on top. Put into an electric cooker.
3. Cover and cook on High 3 to 4 hours.

4 to 6 servings

Cherry Pudding Cake

- **1** can (16 ounces) tart red cherries
- **1** cup sugar
- **1** tablespoon butter or margarine
- **2** eggs
- **1** cup all-purpose flour
- **1** teaspoon baking powder
- **½** teaspoon salt
- **½** cup chopped pecans
- **⅓** cup sugar
- **1** tablespoon cornstarch

1. Drain cherries, reserving juice for sauce.
2. Put 1 cup sugar and butter into a bowl; add eggs, one at a time, beating well after each addition.
3. Mix flour, baking powder, and salt. Add to sugar mixture; mix well. Stir in 1 cup cherries and pecans.
4. Pour batter into a greased and floured 2-pound coffee can. Top with 4 to 6 layers of paper toweling. Set can in an electric cooker. Pour 1½ cups boiling water around can.
5. Cover and cook on High 2 to 4 hours.
6. For sauce, combine remaining sugar and cornstarch in a saucepan. Add reserved cherry juice and remaining cherries. Cook and stir until clear and thickened.
7. Serve pudding cake warm with warm sauce.

6 servings

Blueberry Buckle

- **¼** cup butter or margarine
- **¼** cup sugar
- **1** egg, beaten
- **1** cup all-purpose flour
- **2** teaspoons baking powder
- **¼** cup milk
- **1** pint blueberries, rinsed and drained
- **¼** cup sugar
- **½** cup brown sugar
- **½** cup all-purpose flour
- **½** teaspoon cinnamon
- **¼** cup butter or margarine

1. Cream butter and ¼ cup sugar; beat in egg. Mix flour and baking powder; add alternately with milk to creamed mixture. Turn into a greased and floured cooker bake pan.
2. Sprinkle berries over batter and sprinkle them with ¼ cup sugar.
3. Mix brown sugar, ½ cup flour, cinnamon, and butter. Spoon over fruit. Put lid on bake pan, and set in an electric cooker.
4. Cover and cook on High 3 to 4 hours.
5. Serve warm with **cream** or small scoops of **vanilla ice cream.**

6 servings

Old-fashioned Peach Cobbler

1 cup lightly packed brown sugar
4 teaspoons cornstarch
6 cups sliced fresh peaches
3 whole cloves
1 stick cinnamon
1½ cups all-purpose flour
3 tablespoons sugar
2½ teaspoons baking powder
½ teaspoon salt
⅓ cup chilled butter
1 teaspoon grated lemon peel
¾ cup milk
2 tablespoons brandy (optional)

1. Combine brown sugar and cornstarch in an electric cooker. Add peaches, cloves, and cinnamon; stir.
2. Cover and cook on High 1 to 2 hours, stirring occasionally.
3. Mix flour, sugar, baking powder, and salt in a bowl. Cut in butter until particles are fine. Add lemon peel and milk; mix lightly with a fork until just combined.
4. Remove cover from electric cooker and drop batter by tablespoonfuls onto fruit mixture, spacing evenly.
5. Cover and cook on High 30 minutes.
6. Pour **cream** (mixed with brandy, if desired) over individual servings of warm cobbler.

About 6 servings

Butterscotch Pudding

Batter:
1 cup all-purpose biscuit mix
⅓ cup firmly packed brown sugar
⅓ cup milk
1 teaspoon vanilla extract
½ cup chopped nuts
Topping:
½ cup firmly packed brown sugar
¾ cup boiling water

1. For batter, combine biscuit mix and brown sugar in a bowl. Add milk and vanilla extract. Mix only until smooth. Stir in nuts.
2. Pour batter into a well-greased and floured 1-pound coffee can or cooker bake pan.
3. For topping, combine brown sugar and boiling water. Pour onto batter.
4. Cover coffee can with 6 layers of paper toweling, or, if using bake pan, cover with lid. Set can in electric cooker.
5. Cover and cook on High 2½ hours, or until it springs back when lightly touched.
6. Let stand 10 minutes, then carefully unmold pudding onto a serving dish with sides.
7. Serve pudding warm or cool with whipped topping, if desired.

4 to 6 servings

Mandarin Rice Pudding

2½ cups cooked rice
1 cup undiluted evaporated milk
1 cup drained canned mandarin orange sections (reserve ½ cup syrup)
½ cup packed light brown sugar
3 tablespoons butter or margarine, melted
1 teaspoon vanilla extract
¼ teaspoon orange extract
2 eggs, beaten

1. Put rice, evaporated milk, mandarin orange syrup, brown sugar, butter, extracts, and eggs into an electric cooker; stir thoroughly.
2. Cover and cook on High 2 to 4 hours.
3. Add mandarin oranges to cooker; mix.
4. Cover and cook on High 15 minutes.

About 8 servings

Old-fashioned Rice Pudding

    2½ cups cooked rice
    ⅔   cup sugar
    1   can (13 ounces) evaporated milk
    3   eggs, beaten
    2   teaspoons vanilla extract
    2   tablespoons soft butter
    1   cup golden raisins

1. Put rice and remaining ingredients into a bowl; mix thoroughly.
2. Pour mixture into a buttered electric cooker.
3. Cover and cook on High 1 to 2 hours; stir several times during first 30 minutes.

About 6 servings

Because moisture is captured in the closed cooker, there isn't the evaporation there is in other forms of cooking.

Blueberry Grunt

    2   pints blueberries
    ½   cup water
    ½   cup sugar
    2   cups all-purpose flour
    4   teaspoons baking powder
    1   teaspoon sugar
    ½   teaspoon salt
    1   tablespoon each butter and vegetable
        shortening
    ¾   cup milk (about)

1. Combine berries, water, and sugar in an electric cooker.
2. Cover and cook on High 1 to 2 hours until juice has formed.
3. Mix flour, baking powder, sugar, and salt. Cut in butter and shortening, then, mixing with a fork, add enough milk to make a soft dough.
4. Remove cover from electric cooker and drop batter by tablespoonfuls onto the hot blueberry sauce.
5. Cover and cook on High 15 to 30 minutes.
6. Serve hot with **cream**, if desired.

6 to 8 servings

Cherry-Rhubarb Dessert

    1   pound fresh rhubarb, cut in ¾-inch pieces
    ½   cup sugar
    2   tablespoons flour
    1   cup cherry preserves
    1   cup all-purpose flour
    1   tablespoon sugar
    1½   teaspoons baking powder
    ½   teaspoon salt
    3   tablespoons butter or margarine
    ½   cup milk

1. Put rhubarb in a buttered electric cooker and add ½ cup sugar and 2 tablespoons flour; mix thoroughly. Stir in cherry preserves.
2. Cover and cook on High 2 to 4 hours.
3. Mix remaining flour and sugar with baking powder and salt; cut in butter with pastry blender or 2 knives. Add milk; stir with a fork just until moistened.
4. Remove cover from electric cooker. Spoon topping onto rhubarb.
5. Cover and cook on High 30 minutes.

About 6 servings

Cranberry Pudding with Butter Sauce

    1½   cups all-purpose flour
    ¾   cup sugar
    1   tablespoon baking powder
    3   tablespoons butter, melted
    1½   cups (about 6 ounces) fresh cranberries,
         rinsed and coarsely chopped
    ⅔   cup milk
         Butter Sauce (see below)

1. Mix flour, sugar, and baking powder in a bowl. Make a well in center and add the melted butter, cranberries, and milk. Stir until dry ingredients are moistened.
2. Turn mixture into a greased cooker bake pan and place lid on top. Set pan in an electric cooker.
3. Cover and cook on High 2 to 3 hours. Serve warm with Butter Sauce.

About 6 servings

Butter Sauce: Melt **½ cup butter** in a saucepan. Gradually add **2 cups sugar** and **¾ cup half-and-half,** stirring constantly. Place over low heat and cook, stirring frequently, until sugar is completely dissolved, about 15 minutes. Serve warm.

Indian Pudding

3 cups milk
½ cup yellow cornmeal
¼ cup sugar
1 teaspoon salt
1 teaspoon cinnamon
½ teaspoon ginger
2 eggs, well beaten
½ cup molasses
2 tablespoons butter

1. Scald milk in a heavy saucepan over low heat.
2. Mix cornmeal, sugar, salt, cinnamon, and ginger; stirring constantly, add gradually to scalded milk. Beat egg and molasses together; blend with cornmeal mixture. Cook and stir until thickened, about 10 minutes. Stir in butter.
3. Turn mixture into a small electric cooker.
4. Cover and cook on High 2 to 3 hours until set. Serve warm topped with **ice cream.**

About 6 servings

The moist heat makes ideal conditions to steam puddings. Cake comes out deliciously moist, without ever turning on the oven. Come summer, that's a plus you'll appreciate.

Chunky Applesauce

10 medium cooking apples, pared, cored, and cut in quarters
¾ cup sugar
1 teaspoon cinnamon
½ cup water

1. Put apples into an electric cooker. Mix sugar and cinnamon and sprinkle over apples. Pour in water.
2. Cover and cook on High 2 to 4 hours.

6 servings

Rosé Baked Apples

5 Rome Beauty or Golden Delicious apples
3 strips orange peel
¼ cup orange juice
1 cup rosé wine
¼ teaspoon nutmeg
½ cup lightly packed light brown sugar
Whipped cream or ice cream for topping

1. Core apples and pare each about a quarter of the way down. Arrange in a large electric cooker.
2. Combine orange peel, juice, wine, nutmeg, and brown sugar and pour over apples.
3. Cover and cook on Low 3 to 4 hours.
4. Serve warm or cold with wine sauce; top with whipped cream or ice cream.

5 baked apples

Stuffed Baked Apples

6 to 8 baking apples, cored (do not pare)
½ cup lightly packed brown sugar
¼ cup raisins
½ cup chopped pecans
Red cinnamon candies
½ cup water
Miniature marshmallows

1. Put cored apples into a large electric cooker.
2. Mix brown sugar, raisins, and pecans; fill apple centers.
3. Add cinnamon candies and water to cooker. Place several miniature marshmallows on top of apples.
4. Cover and cook on Low 3 to 4 hours.

6 to 8 servings

Apricot-Wine Compote

12 ounces dried apricots
½ cup golden raisins
¼ cup lightly packed brown sugar
2½ cups water
½ cup dry sherry
¼ cup lemon juice
Vanilla ice cream
¼ cup slivered toasted almonds

1. Put apricots, raisins, brown sugar, water, sherry, and lemon juice into an electric cooker.
2. Cover and cook on Low 4 to 5 hours.
3. Serve warm or cold spooned over vanilla ice cream and sprinkled with almonds.

About 6 servings

Candied Bananas

6 green-tipped bananas, peeled
½ cup flaked coconut
½ teaspoon cinnamon
¼ teaspoon salt
½ cup dark corn syrup
¼ cup butter or margarine, melted
2 teaspoons grated lemon peel
¼ cup lemon juice

1. Put bananas and coconut into a large electric cooker. Sprinkle with cinnamon and salt.
2. Mix corn syrup, butter, lemon peel, and lemon juice; pour over bananas.
3. Cover and cook on Low 1 to 2 hours.

6 servings

Poached Pears in Port

6 ripe pears, pared
2 cups port wine
2 cups sugar
4 thin strips lemon peel
Pistachio nuts

1. Arrange pears upright in an electric cooker.
2. Combine wine, sugar, and lemon peel; pour over pears.

3. Cover and cook on High 2 to 4 hours; turn pears occasionally and baste with wine sauce.
4. Serve warm or chilled; sprinkle with pistachio nuts.

About 6 servings

Cinnamon Pears

6 fresh pears
2 tablespoons butter or margarine
¾ cup lightly packed brown sugar
1 teaspoon cinnamon
¼ cup water

1. Core pears; place upright in a large electric cooker. Dot with butter.
2. Combine brown sugar and cinnamon; sprinkle over pears. Pour in water.
3. Cover and cook on High 1 to 2 hours.
4. Serve pears warm in syrup, or chilled with **cream.**

6 servings

Gingered Prunes

3 cups dried prunes
2 lemons, cut in thin slices
2 cups sugar
½ cup finely sliced preserved ginger
5 cups water

1. Put prunes, lemon slices, sugar, and ginger into an electric cooker. Pour water over all.
2. Cover and cook on High 1 to 2 hours.

6 to 8 servings

Springtime Rhubarb Ambrosia

2 pounds tender pink rhubarb, cut in 1-inch pieces (6 to 8 cups)
1½ cups sugar
½ teaspoon cinnamon
2 teaspoons grated lemon peel
4 teaspoons lemon juice

1. Toss rhubarb with sugar, cinnamon, and lemon peel; turn into an electric cooker. Drizzle with lemon juice.
2. Cover and cook on High 1 to 2 hours.

8 to 10 servings

Curried Fruit Medley

1 can (16 ounces) cling peach halves, drained
1 can (15 ounces) pineapple slices, drained
1 can (16 ounces) whole apricots, drained
1 can (16 ounces) pear halves, drained
1 cup maraschino cherries, drained
⅓ cup firmly packed light brown sugar
2 cinnamon sticks
6 whole cloves
½ teaspoon curry powder
1 cup dry white wine

1. Put peaches, pineapple, apricots, pears, and maraschino cherries in electric cooker.
2. Blend brown sugar, cinnamon, cloves, and curry powder. Combine with wine; pour over fruit.
3. Cover and cook on High 1 to 2 hours.

About 10 servings

Homemade Mincemeat

1 pound cooked lean roast beef, cut in pieces
½ pound suet
5 pounds tart apples
½ pound seedless raisins, chopped
1 pound dried currants
¼ pound candied citron, chopped
¼ pound candied orange peel, chopped
2 tablespoons grated orange peel
1 tablespoon grated lemon peel
¼ cup orange juice
2 tablespoons lemon juice
2 cups sugar
1 teaspoon cinnamon
½ teaspoon cloves
½ teaspoon nutmeg
½ teaspoon mace
½ teaspoon powdered coriander seed
1 teaspoon salt
½ teaspoon pepper
2 cups apple cider
1 can (16 ounces) tart red cherries
    (undrained)
½ pound walnuts, coarsely chopped
1 cup brandy

1. Finely chop meat and beef suet or put through coarse blade of food chopper, and put into a large electric cooker.
2. Wash, quarter, core, and pare the apples;

coarsely chop or put through coarse blade of a food chopper (there should be about 6 cups chopped).
3. Add apples and all other ingredients, except nuts and brandy, to cooker; stir.
4. Cover and cook on High 4 to 6 hours, stirring occasionally.
5. Stir in nuts.
6. Cover and cook on High 15 to 30 minutes.
7. Stir in brandy. Quickly ladle the mincemeat into hot, sterilized jars; seal.

About 7 (1-pint) jars

Cooker Fruit Topping

1 can (29 ounces) sliced cling peaches
1 can (20 ounces) pineapple chunks
3 tablespoons butter, softened
1 teaspoon grated lemon peel
½ cup currant jelly
¼ cup coconut

1. Drain peaches and pineapple and put into an electric cooker.
2. Combine butter, lemon peel, currant jelly, and coconut. Pour over fruit in cooker.
3. Cover and cook on High 1 to 2 hours.
4. Spoon over ice cream or pudding.

8 servings

Crockery Chutney

1 quart diced pared tart apples
1 cup finely chopped onion
1 cup dark seedless raisins
1 cup golden raisins
1 cup currants
½ cup sugar
1 teaspoon salt
1½ teaspoons ginger
½ teaspoon allspice
⅛ teaspoon cloves
1 cup vinegar
1 cup dry white wine or water
¼ cup diced green pepper
¼ cup diced pimento

1. Combine all ingredients, except green pepper and pimento, in a large electric cooker.
2. Cover and cook on High 2 to 4 hours.
3. Add green pepper and pimento to cooker; stir.
4. Cover and cook on High 30 minutes.

About 1½ quarts chutney

BEVERAGES

The King likes a cocktail
Or two before dinner;
But the Princess sips wine
As befits a beginner!

ANON

Dressy Tea

½ cup sugar
4 whole cloves
1 stick cinnamon
2 teaspoons instant tea
1 cup orange juice
1 quart boiling water
  Lemon slices

1. Combine sugar, spices, tea, and orange juice in an electric cooker. Pour in boiling water and stir to combine ingredients thoroughly.
2. Cover and cook on Low 1 to 2 hours.
3. At serving time, ladle into teacups and garnish with lemon slices.

About 6 servings

Hot Ginger Tea

4 teaspoons instant tea
2 sticks cinnamon
4 whole cloves
2 large pieces crystallized ginger, cut in very thin slices
3 tablespoons sugar
1½ quarts boiling water
  Orange

1. Combine tea, spices, and sugar in an electric cooker. Pour in boiling water and stir well.
2. Cover and cook on Low 1 to 2 hours.
3. Slice orange and cut slices into quarters.
4. To serve, ladle tea into cups and float one or two quarter-slices of orange in each.

About 8 servings

Party Coffee

3 sticks cinnamon
6 whole cloves
8 cups (coffee-cup size) hot coffee
  Sweetened whipped cream

1. Combine cinnamon sticks, cloves, and coffee in an electric cooker.
2. Cover and cook on Low 1 to 2 hours.
3. At serving time, ladle into coffee cups. Accompany with a bowl of sweetened whipped cream.

8 servings

Spiced Coffee with Brandy

8 cups (coffee-cup size) hot coffee
8 whole cloves
8 whole allspice
2 sticks cinnamon
2 strips lemon peel (use colored part only, white is bitter)
1 strip orange peel (use colored part only, white is bitter)
1 cup brandy

1. Put hot coffee, spices, and fruit peels into an electric cooker; mix thoroughly.
2. Cover and cook on Low 2 hours. At serving time, discard peels and whole spices.
3. Put 2 tablespoons brandy into each coffee cup and fill with hot spiced coffee.

About 8 servings

Café l'Orange

2 medium oranges, sliced
  Whole cloves
8 cups (coffee-cup size) hot coffee
  Sweetened whipped cream
  Brown sugar
  Ground cinnamon

1. Stud each orange slice with 3 whole cloves; put into an electric cooker and pour hot coffee over them.
2. Cover and cook on Low 1 to 2 hours. Discard orange slices and cloves.
3. At serving time, ladle coffee into cups. Accompany with bowls of whipped cream and brown sugar, and a shaker of cinnamon, so that guests may flavor their coffee as desired.

8 servings

Wassail

    3 cups water
    ½ cup orange juice
    ¼ cup lemon juice
    3 whole oranges, studded with cloves (see
        Note)
 1½ teaspoons whole allspice
    2 sticks cinnamon
    ¼ teaspoon nutmeg
    ¼ teaspoon ginger
    2 cups water
    ¾ cup sugar
    ¼ cup instant tea
    ½ gallon apple cider

1. Combine 3 cups water, orange juice, lemon juice, 1 studded orange, and spices in an electric cooker.
2. Cover and cook on Low 2½ hours.
3. Bake the remaining studded oranges in a 350°F oven 45 minutes; reserve until serving time.
4. Meanwhile, stir 2 cups water into sugar in a saucepan; bring to boiling, stirring only until sugar dissolves, and boil 5 minutes.
5. Add sugar syrup, instant tea, and apple cider to spiced fruit juice mixture in electric cooker.
6. Cover and cook on Low 15 to 30 minutes, or until heated through.
7. Strain, transfer to punch bowl, pierce baked oranges several times with wooden pick, float them in wassail, and serve in punch cups. Make sure that bowl and punch cups are heatproof.

About 3½ quarts punch

Note: To stud oranges, pierce with wooden pick at 1-inch intervals and insert cloves.

Hot Apricot Nip

    2 cans (12 ounces each) apricot nectar
    2 cups water
    ¼ cup lemon juice
    ¼ cup sugar
    2 whole cloves
    2 sticks cinnamon

1. Put all ingredients into an electric cooker; stir to combine thoroughly.
2. Cover and cook on Low 2 hours, or until as hot as desired.
3. Remove spices; ladle into mugs.

About 8 servings

Buttered Rum Punch

    2 quarts apple cider
    ½ cup lightly packed brown sugar
    ¼ cup butter, melted
 1½ cups dark rum
    Cinnamon

1. Put cider, brown sugar, and butter into an electric cooker; stir to mix thoroughly.
2. Cover and cook on Low 2 hours.
3. Stir in rum.
4. Cover and cook on Low 15 to 30 minutes, or until as hot as desired.
5. Ladle into heatproof punch cups and sprinkle with cinnamon.

12 servings

After you get the hang of crock cooking, you will probably want to adapt some of your own favorite recipes to it.

Hot Spiced Cider

    2   quarts apple cider
    ⅓   cup lightly packed brown sugar
    2   sticks cinnamon
    1   teaspoon whole cloves
    1   teaspoon whole allspice

1. Put ingredients into an electric cooker; stir to mix thoroughly.
2. Cover and cook on Low 2 hours, or until as hot as desired.
3. Serve hot in mugs.

About 2 quarts spiced cider

The slow cooker is a handy hostess tool; it doubles as a keep-warm serving dish. At holiday time a pot of wassail or mulled wine can simmer away on the buffet without taking up precious space on the range top.

Hot Buttered Cranberry Punch

    1½ cups water
    ⅔   cup firmly packed brown sugar
    ½   teaspoon cinnamon
    ¼   teaspoon allspice
    ⅛   teaspoon cloves
    ⅛   teaspoon nutmeg
    ⅛   teaspoon salt
    1   can (18 ounces) unsweetened pineapple
          juice
    2   cups water
    4   cups fresh cranberries, rinsed and sorted
          Butter or margarine

1. Combine 1½ cups water, brown sugar, spices, and salt in a saucepan. Bring to boiling. Reduce heat and simmer 5 minutes.
2. Transfer mixture to an electric cooker. Add pineapple juice.
3. Cover and cook on Low 2 hours.
4. Meanwhile, bring 2 cups water to boiling in a saucepan. Add cranberries and cook, uncovered, until the skins pop.
5. Force cranberries through a food mill or sieve to make a purée. Stir purée into mixture in electric cooker.

6. Cover and cook on Low 15 to 30 minutes to combine flavors.
7. Ladle punch into serving cups or mugs and add dots of butter to each cup. Serve with cinnamon stick stirrers, if desired.

About 1½ quarts punch

Mulled Wine

    1   can (46 ounces) pineapple juice
    2   cans (6 ounces each) frozen orange juice
          concentrate, reconstituted as directed
    1½ cups water
    1   cup sugar
    3   lemons, sliced
    3   sticks cinnamon
    3   tablespoons whole cloves
    3   bottles (⅘ quart each) dry red wine

1. Combine pineapple juice and orange juice in a large electric cooker.
2. Cover and cook on Low 1 to 2 hours.
3. Boil water with sugar, lemons, cinnamon, and spices in a saucepan 5 minutes.
4. Strain syrup and add to mixture in cooker with wine.
5. Cover and cook on Low 1 hour, or until as hot as desired.
6. Ladle into cups.

About 5 quarts mulled wine

Mulled Grapefruit Punch

   1 **can (46 ounces) unsweetened grapefruit juice**
   1 **cup canned apricot nectar**
   1 **cup water**
1⅓ **cups sugar**
   1 **teaspoon whole cloves**
   2 **sticks cinnamon**

1. Put all ingredients into an electric cooker; stir to mix thoroughly.
2. Cover and cook on Low 2 hours, or until as hot as desired.
3. Ladle into mugs.

About 2 quarts punch

Herb-Buttered Hot Tomato Juice

  1 **can (46 ounces) tomato juice**
  1 **teaspoon Worcestershire sauce**
½ **teaspoon salt**
¼ **teaspoon marjoram leaves, crushed**
¼ **teaspoon oregano leaves, crushed**
  4 **whole cloves**
¼ **cup butter or margarine**

1. Put tomato juice, Worcestershire sauce, salt, marjoram, oregano, and cloves into an electric cooker; stir to combine thoroughly.
2. Cover and cook on Low 2 hours, or until as hot as desired.
3. Remove cloves. Add butter and stir until melted. Serve at once.

About 6 cups

Sherried Bouillon

  2 **cans (about 10 ounces each) condensed beef broth**
  1 **cup boiling water**
  2 **tablespoons lemon juice**
    Sherry

1. Combine beef broth, water, and lemon juice in electric cooker. Cover and cook on Low 1 to 2 hours.
2. At serving time, ladle into mugs and add desired amount of sherry to each serving.

About 6 servings

Hot Aromatic Punch

¼ **cup sugar**
  5 **teaspoons instant tea**
  2 **teaspoons ground sage**
  1 **quart apple cider**
4½ **cups boiling water**

1. Put all ingredients into an electric cooker; stir to combine thoroughly.
2. Cover and cook on Low about 2 hours, or until as hot as desired.
3. Serve hot in mugs. Garnish each with a twist of lemon, if desired.

About 2 quarts punch

Sage-Cider Punch

  1 **quart apple cider**
  1 **cup sugar**
  2 **tablespoons lime juice (juice of 1 small lime)**
  1 **teaspoon ground sage**
  1 **teaspoon instant tea**

1. Put all ingredients into an electric cooker; stir to mix thoroughly.
2. Cover and cook on Low 2 hours, or until as hot as desired.
3. Ladle into punch cups.

About 1½ quarts punch

INDEX

Applesauce cake, 85

Beef
  and kidney beans southwestern style, 34
  -and-rice stuffed peppers, 39
  bourguignon, 59
  burgoo, 35
  Burgundy style, 32
  chili
    and beans, 38
    con carne, 37
  cola steak, 59
  cooker corned, 59
  dip, hot cheese 'n', 39
  ground meat in barbecue sauce, 65
  Hungarian goulash (Gulyáshus), 59
  in savory sauce, 58
  lima bean chili con carne, 38
  meat and cabbage, 40
  meatballs
    in apple-tomato sauce, 64
    saucy, 63
    Swedish, 64
  meat loaf
    surprise, 63
    walnut, 63
  picadillo, 64
  pot roast, 58
    savory, 58
    teriyaki, 58
    with vegetables, 34
  sauerbraten, 51
  short ribs
    fruity, 60
    spiced, with cabbage, 36
    western style, 36
  soup, *see* Soups
  Spanish rice, 38
  stew, *see* Stews
  strips, spicy, 60
Beverages, 97
  coffee
    café l'orange, 98
    party, 98
    with brandy, spiced, 98
  herb-buttered hot tomato juice, 101
  hot apricot nip, 99
  hot spiced cider, 100
  mulled wine, 100
  punch
    buttered rum, 99
    hot aromatic, 101

  hot buttered cranberry, 100
  mulled grapefruit, 101
  sage-cider, 101
  sherried bouillon, 101
  tea
    dressy, 98
    hot ginger, 98
  wassail, 99
Bologna stew, 48
Borsch with beef, hot, 14
Bouillabaisse, 70
Breads, 79
  apricot-nut, 81
  Boston brown, 82
  cheerie cherry, 82
  cranberry fruit-nut, 80
  gingerbread, 81
  Irish soda, with currants, 80
  lemon-saffron, 82
  nutty orange-date, 81
  oatmeal-raisin, 80
  pudding, 89
  spoonbread, 82

Cakes, *see* Desserts
Carbonada criolla, 53
Casserole(s)
  one-cook, 35
  pork chop, 42
Chicken
  à la king, 69
  and dumplings, 68
  casa, 69
  coq au vin, 66
  country captain, 65
  fricassee with vegetables, 66
  hunter style, 68
  in tomato sauce (pollo Madrileño), 67
  kumquat, 68
  slowpoke, 69
  soup, *see* Soups
  spicy cooker, 67
  stew, *see* Stews
  Texas-style barbecued, 66
  with rice, 45
Chili
  and beans, 38
  con carne, 37
  lima bean chili con carne, 38
Chowder
  Brussels sprout, 28
  Pacific seafood, 21
  salmon, 22
Coq au vin, 66
Corned beef, cooker, 59
Court bouillon, white wine, 21

Desserts, 83
  apple-cheese betty, 90
  apple-lemon brown betty, 91
  apricot-wine compote, 94

  blueberry buckle, 91
  blueberry grunt, 93
  cakes
    apple, 85
    applesauce, 85
    bishop's, 87
    California orange-date, 84
    cherry pudding, 91
    crockery wallbanger, 84
    flowerpot banana, 86
    nut pound, 86
    super turban, 85
    vanilla wafer, 84
  candied bananas, 95
  cherry-rhubarb, 93
  chunky applesauce, 94
  cinnamon pears, 95
  cooker fruit topping, 96
  crockery chutney, 96
  crockery fruitcake, 86
  curried fruit medley, 96
  gingered prunes, 95
  homemade mincemeat, 96
  old-fashioned peach cobbler, 92
  poached pears in port, 95
  puddings
    bread, 89
    butterscotch, 92
    chocolate nut, 88
    cranberry, with butter sauce, 93
    Indian, 94
    mandarin rice, 92
    old-fashioned rice, 93
    orange marmalade, 89
    plum, 88
    steamed carrot, 90
    steamed chocolate, 90
    steamed date, 87
    steamed pumpkin, 88
    steamed raisin, 89
  rosé baked apples, 94
  springtime rhubarb ambrosia, 95
  stuffed baked apples, 94
Dip, hot cheese 'n' beef, 39
Dolmas, 52
Dumplings
  basil, 68
  beef stew with, 33
  chicken and, 68

Escarole soup, 17

Fish, see specific kinds
Fisherman's stew, 47
Fondue, cheesy tuna-onion, 46
Frankfurters
  beans and, 47
  lentil soup with, 25
Fruits
  apples
    rosé baked, 94
    stuffed baked, 94

candied bananas, 95
chunky applesauce, 94
cinnamon pears, 95
crockery chutney, 96
gingered prunes, 95
medley, curried, 96
poached pears in port, 95
topping, cooker, 96

Glaze, 85
Glaze, chocolate, 85
Goulash
  Hungarian (Gulyáshus), 59
  szekely, 44
  vegetable, 78
Gumbo
  creamy creole, 20
  filé, 20

Ham
  'n' cabbage dinner, 44
  -vegetable soup, 15
  with apricot glaze, buffet, 62
Herb bouquet, 40

Know Your Cooker, 9
  cooking with the crock, 10
    converting recipes, 11
    selecting recipes, 11
  features of the slow cooker, 9
  techniques with the crock, 11
    after the lid comes off, 12
    before the lid goes on, 11
    during cooking, 12
  use and care, 10
    before you cook, 10
    play it safe, 10

Lamb
  couscous, 41
  shanks, lemon, 60
  stew
    favorite, 40
    Irish, 41
Lentil
  soup, turkey-, 18
  soup with frankfurters, 25

Main Dishes, 31–48
Meatballs
  in apple-tomato sauce, 64
  saucy, 63
  soup with, 18
  Swedish, 64
Meat loaf
  surprise, 63
  walnut, 63
Meat, Poultry, and Fish, 57–70
Mincemeat, homemade, 96
Mulligatawny soup, 56

Oriental meat and vegetable stew, 55
Oxtail
  soup, 16
  soup paprikash, 16
  stew, 34

Passport to International Culinary Adventure, 49
  Argentina, 53
  China/U.S.A., 55
  France/Italy, 49
  Germany, 51
  India/England, 56
  Soviet Union, 54
  Turkey, 52
  Yugoslavia, 50
Pollo Madrileño (chicken in tomato sauce), 67
Pork
  chop(s)
    casserole, 42
    chicken lickin'-good, 60
    fresh pear and, skillet, 61
    -vegetable supper, 42
    with apples, baked kraut and, 41
  ribs
    and kraut, oven, 43
    barbecued country, 62
    saucy, 62
  schnitz un knepp (apples and buttons), 42
  smoked shoulder roll and beans, 44
  sweet and pungent, 61
  szekely goulash, 44
  with herbs, spicy, 61
Poultry, see specific kinds
Puddings, see Desserts

Rabbit stew, 45
Red snapper soup, 20
Rice
  beef-and-, stuffed peppers, 39
  chicken with, 45
  medley, vegetable-, 77
  pudding
    mandarin, 92
    old-fashioned, 93
Spanish, 38

Salmon chowder, 22
Sataras, 50
Sauce(s)
  apple-tomato, meatballs in, 64
  barbecue, ground meat in, 65
  brown sugar pudding, 89
  butter, 93
  cheese, cauliflower with, 75

hard, 87
horseradish, 15
horseradish cream, broccoli with, 73
Italian spaghetti, 36
lemony meat, with spaghetti, 37
lemon zest crème, 88
orange, beets in, 73
ripe olive, asparagus in, 72
savory, beef in, 58
spaghetti, 36
special brown, 21
thick white, 29
tomato, chicken in (pollo Madrileño), 67
vanilla, 89
Sauerbraten, 51
Sauerkraut
  baked kraut and chops with apples, 41
  oven ribs and kraut, 43
  with apples, 76
  with caraway, 76
Sausage soup Italiano, 17
Schnitz un knepp (apples and buttons), 42
Short ribs
  fruity, 60
  spiced, with cabbage, 36
  western style, 36
Shrimp
  creole, 70
  jambalaya, 46
Solianka, 54
Soup(s), 13
  bean, 22
    barley, and sausage, 23
    black, 22
    garbanzo, -salami, 24
    Greek, 23
    lima, bisque, 23
  beef
    encore, 15
    hot borsch with, 14
    Norwegian vegetable, with, 15
    stock, 14
    vegetable-, 16
  black mushroom-wine, 26
  borsch with beef, hot, 14
  cabbage, 14
  cheese, 30
  chicken
    -corn, 19
    country-style, 19
    -noodle, 19
    -vegetable, 19
  chili-potato, 30
  chowder
    Brussels sprout, 28
    Pacific seafood, 21
    salmon, 22
  cream of fresh mushroom, 26

cream of potato-leek, 29
creamy carrot, 26
escarole, 17
French-Canadian onion, 27
gumbo
   creamy creole, 20
   filé, 20
ham-vegetable, 15
harvest, 30
kettle supper, 25
lentil, with frankfurters, 25
macaroni-tuna, 21
Mexicana, 18
mixed fruit, 30
mulligatawny, 56
oxtail, 16
oxtail, paprikash, 16
pea
   à la francaise, 29
   blender, 24
   split, 24
   split, -vegetable, 24
   yellow, with pork, 25
red snapper, 20
sausage, Italiano, 17
solianka, 54
spiced fresh tomato cream, 28
squash, 27
turkey-lentil, 18
vegetable
   -beef, 16
   chicken-, 19
   Dutch, 15
   easy, 27
   ham-, 15
   Italienne, 28
   minestrone style, 17
   Norwegian, with beef, 15
   split pea-, 24
   with meatballs, 18
Spaghetti
   lemony meat sauce with, 37
   sauce, 36

sauce, Italian, 36
Stews
  beef
    barley, 39
    homestyle, 33
    multi-vegetable, 32
    stifado, 33
    vegetable, 32
    with dumplings, 33
  bologna, 48
  carbonada criolla, 53
  favorite lamb, 40
  fisherman's, 47
  Irish, 41
  oriental meat and vegetable, 55
  oxtail, 34
  rabbit, 45
  sataras, 50
  versatile tomato-celery, 43
Stifado, 33
Stuffed peppers
  beef-and-rice, 39
  dolmas, 52
  turkey-, 45
Swedish meatballs, 64
Szekely goulash, 44

Tripe creole, 46
Tuna
  -onion fondue, cheesy, 46
  soup, macaroni-, 21
Turkey
  legs, barbecued, 70
  -lentil soup, 18
  roast stuffed, 69
  -stuffed peppers, 45

Veal
  carbonada criolla, 53
  loaf, skillet, 65
  one-cook casserole, 35

Vegetable(s), 71
acorn squash stuffed with corn, 77
asparagus in ripe olive sauce, 72
bean(s)
  and franks, 47
  buckaroo, 47
  creamy green, 72
  creamy molasses limas, 78
  crockery lima, 78
  green, with water chestnuts, 73
  old-fashioned green, with bacon, 72
  pot, barbecue, 48
  sweet-and-sour green, with bananas, 72
beets in orange sauce, 73
broccoli with horseradish cream, 73
cabbage
  company, 74
  red, Danish style, 74
cauliflower with cheese sauce, 75
cooker carrots, 75
goulash, 78
peas
  easy black-eye, 78
  with sweet basil, 75
potatoes
  Anna, 76
  Dutch stewed, 76
  scalloped, 76
  scalloped sweet, and apples, 77
-rice medley, 77
sauerkraut
  baked kraut and chops with apples, 41
  oven ribs and kraut, 43
  with apples, 76
  with caraway, 76
savory Brussels sprouts, 74
soup, *see* Soups
spiced spinach, 77
stew, *see* Stews

Capstone   2/20/14   19.99

PETS' GUIDES

Nibble's Guide to

Caring for Your Hamster

Anita Ganeri

Heinemann
LIBRARY

Chicago, Illinois

Edited by Daniel Nunn, Rebecca Rissman, and Sian Smith
Designed by Cynthia Della-Rovere
Original illustrations © Capstone Global Library Ltd 2013
Illustrated by Rick Peterson
Picture research by Tracy Cummins
Production by Victoria Fitzgerald
Originated by Capstone Global Library Ltd
Printed in the United States of America in North Mankato, Minnesota. 122013   007920RP

17 16 15 14 13
10 9 8 7 6 5 4 3

Library of Congress Cataloging-in-Publication Data

Ganeri, Anita, 1961-
Nibble's guide to caring for your hamster / Anita Ganeri.
    p. cm.—(Pets' guides)
Includes bibliographical references and index.
ISBN 978-1-4329-7133-5 (hb)—ISBN 978-1-4329-7140-3 (pb) 1. Hamsters as pets—Juvenile literature. I. Title.
SF459.H3G347 2013
636.935—dc23   2012017281

Acknowledgments

The author and publisher are grateful to the following for permission to reproduce copyright material: Alamy pp. 13 (© Top-Pet-Pics), 21 (© Papilio), 23 (© Top-Pet-Pics); Biosphoto p. 5 (Michel Gunther); Capstone Library pp. 7, 11, 15, 17, 25 (Karon Dubke); iStockphoto pp. 19 (© Daniel Juhl Mogensen), 27 (© Andres Balcazar); Shutterstock p. 9 (© Victoria Rak @Tuff Photo).

Cover photograph of a black-bellied hamster reproduced with permission of Superstock (© age fotostock). Design elements reproduced with permission of Shutterstock (© Picsfive) and Shutterstock (© R-studio).

We would like to thank Teresa Linford (Mad About Hamsters) for her invaluable help in the preparation of this book.

Every effort has been made to contact copyright holders of any material reproduced in this book. Any omissions will be rectified in subsequent printings if notice is given to the publisher.

All the Internet addresses (URLs) given in this book were valid at the time of going to press. However, due to the dynamic nature of the Internet, some addresses may have changed, or sites may have changed or ceased to exist since publication. While the author and publisher regret any inconvenience this may cause readers, no responsibility for any such changes can be accepted by either the author or the publisher.

Contents

Do You Want a Pet Hamster? 4

Choosing Your Hamster 6

A Healthy Hamster. 8

Getting Ready 10

My New Home 12

Coming Home 14

Dinner Time 16

Time for Play 18

Cleaning My Cage 20

Teeth and Fur. 22

Visiting the Vet 24

Vacation Care 26

Hamster Facts 28

Helpful Tips 29

Glossary 30

Find Out More 31

Index 32

Some words are shown in bold, **like this**. You can find out what they mean by looking in the glossary.

Do You Want a Pet Hamster?

Hi! I'm Nibble the hamster, and I'm very happy to meet you. Did you know that hamsters like me make great pets? We're clean, friendly, and very easy to look after. We're also fun to keep.

You'll need to be a good pet owner and look after me properly. I'll need food, water, and a clean, safe place to live. Then I'll quickly become your best friend.

Choosing Your Hamster

There are lots of different types of hamsters you can choose from. I'm a golden hamster. I get my name from the color of my fur. Golden hamsters like me are happy living on our own. We don't like living with other hamsters.

These hamsters are babies and will soon need to live alone.

You can buy a hamster from a pet shop or go to an animal shelter. Animal shelters often have hamsters that need good, new homes.

A Healthy Hamster

Pick a hamster that looks happy and healthy, just like me! Look at my round body, soft, shiny fur, and bright, clear eyes. I'm your perfect pet!

Your new pet should be lively and nosy. I'm always scurrying around. A hamster that's scared or crouching in a corner may not be well.

Getting Ready

Before you bring me home, there are a few things that you need to get ready. Here is my hamster homecoming shopping list…

Nibble's Shopping List

- 🐾 a large cage with a **nest box**
- 🐾 **shredded** tissue paper or hay for bedding
- 🐾 wood shavings for the floor of the cage
- 🐾 an exercise wheel
- 🐾 a **drip-feeder** water bottle
- 🐾 a food bowl
- 🐾 hamster food

My New Home

Like all hamsters, I love climbing and running around. Please make sure that you get me a big cage with plenty of room and a cozy **nest box** for sleeping in.

Put my cage somewhere safe and warm, but out of bright sunlight and away from chilly **drafts**. Make sure that the door closes properly. I'm smart at escaping!

Coming Home

You can carry me home in a small cardboard box with holes so that I can breathe. At home, put me in my cage. I might be shy at first, so leave me alone for a few hours to settle in.

Give me a gentle stroke at first so that I get used to being **handled**. Later, you can pick me up by scooping me up gently in both hands. Let me climb from one of your hands to the other. Talk to me softly so that I don't feel frightened.

Dinner Time

It's dinner time and I'm hungry! I like to have one meal a day, in the evening. Don't worry if I store some of my food in the **pouches** in my cheeks. I'm saving it to eat later!

Nibble the Hamster's Top Meal-Time Tips

 Feed me a mixture of seeds, nuts, and **grains**. You can buy special hamster food from a pet shop.

 Put my food in a heavy dish so that it doesn't tip over.

 Keep my water bottle filled up with fresh water.

Time for Play

Hamsters like me need lots of exercise and chances to play. Otherwise, we quickly get bored and unhappy. Cardboard tubes and glass jars make great hamster toys.

You can also put an exercise wheel in my cage. Make sure that it's solid so I don't get my feet trapped. Then I can go for a run at night—that's when I'm wide awake.

Cleaning My Cage

Please keep my cage nice and clean. Otherwise, I might get sick. Every day, take away any **droppings** and pieces of old food. Wash out my food bowl and water bottle.

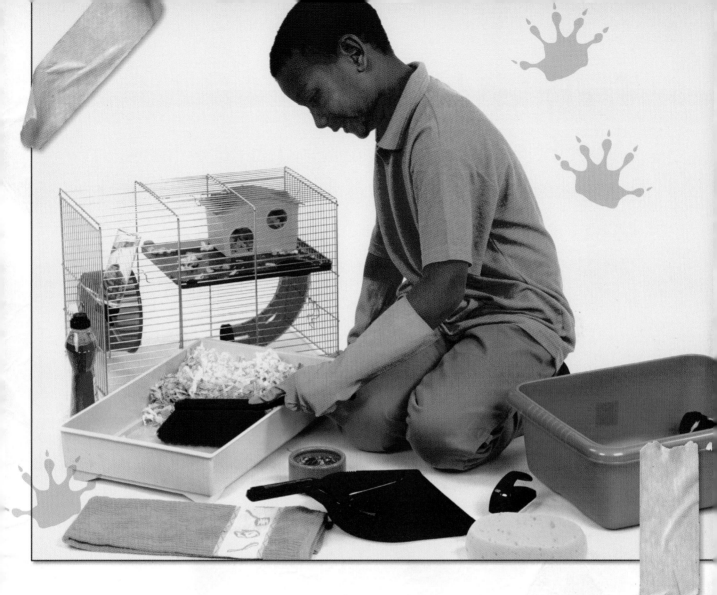

Once a week, you need to clean my whole cage out. Put fresh bedding in my **nest box** and fresh wood shavings on the floor. Don't forget to wash your hands afterward.

Teeth and Fur

My front teeth keep growing all the time. I'm very used to that. But if they get too long, I can't eat properly. Please give me a wooden **gnawing** block to wear my teeth down.

You can groom your hamster with its own soft toothbrush.

I have short fur so I can **groom** it with my front paws to keep it clean and glossy. If you have a long-haired hamster, you need to groom it every other day with a soft brush.

Visiting the Vet

Hamsters like me will stay fit and healthy if you take good care of us. If I don't look well, take me to the vet. Just like you, I can catch colds and the flu—AAATCHOOO!

There are other signs that show you that I'm not feeling very well. Take me to the vet if my breathing sounds noisy, my eyes are cloudy, my bottom is dirty, or I stop eating my food.

Vacation Care

Don't just go away and leave me when you go on vacation. I still need food, fresh water, and clean bedding, so ask a friend or neighbor to take care of me.

Take me to a friend's house or tell someone to stop in every day. It's a good idea to leave plenty of supplies and a list of what the person needs to do. Then your friend or neighbor won't forget anything.

Hamster Facts

- Wild hamsters live in the desert. They sleep in **burrows** that they dig deep underground. This helps to keep them cool.

- Wild hamsters eat a mixture of seeds, **grains**, insects such as crickets, and baby insects.

- Hamsters cannot see very well. They use their whiskers to help them find their way around.

- Hamsters usually live for about two years, though some can live longer.

Helpful Tips

- Use wood shavings instead of sawdust in your hamster's cage. Sawdust is very fine and may irritate your hamster's nose.

- Every few days, give your hamster a tiny piece of fruit or vegetable as a treat. Don't feed your hamster oranges, lemons, onions, grapes, or rhubarb.

- A good way of letting your hamster get to know you is to sit in a dry bathtub. Then let your hamster climb over you.

- Never leave your hamster alone with another animal, even if they seem like good friends. Other animals might frighten or harm your hamster.

Glossary

burrows holes that hamsters and other animals dig in the ground to live in

drafts blasts of cold air that come through windows or under doors

drip-feeder a bottle that is attached to a hamster's cage and lets water slowly drip out

droppings hamster poo

gnawing a way of chewing and biting

grains food such as corn or wheat that comes from plants

groom to brush and clean a hamster's fur. Hamsters also groom their own fur.

handled when a hamster is picked up and stroked

nest box a box that is filled with soft bedding for a hamster to sleep in

pouches spaces inside a hamster's cheeks where it stores pieces of food

shredded paper that has been torn into lots of small pieces

Find Out More

Books

Landau, Elaine. *Your Pet Hamster*. New York:
 Scholastic, 2007.

Richardson, Adele D. *Caring for Your Hamster*.
 Mankato, Minn.: Capstone, 2007.

Tourville, Amanda Doering. *Skitter and Scoot: Bringing
 Home a Hamster*. Mankato, Minn.: Capstone, 2009.

Internet Sites

Facthound offers a safe, fun way to
find Internet sites related to this book.
All of the sites on Facthound have been
researched by our staff.

Here's all you do: Visit www.facthound.com
Type in this code: 9781432971335

Index

animal shelters 7

bedding 11, 21
bringing your hamster home
    14–15
buying your hamster 7

cage 11, 12–13, 14, 20–21
choosing your hamster 6–7
cleaning the cage 20–1

droppings 20

exercise wheel 11, 19

facts and tips 28–29
food and water 16–17, 28, 29
fur 6, 8, 23

gnawing block 22
golden hamsters 6
grooming 23

handling your hamster 15
healthy hamsters 8–9
homecoming checklist
    10–11

illness 9, 24–25

nest box 11, 12, 21

other pets 29

play 18–19
pouches 16

teeth 22
toys 18
treats 29

vacation care 26–27
vet 24, 25

water bottle 11, 17, 20
wild hamsters 28
wood shavings 11, 29